SHAPING THE FUTURE

contributors

JOHN McHALE
NORMAN E. BORLAUG
ANTHONY J. WIENER
JOSEPH SITTLER
GLENN T. SEABORG

Shaping the Future

A DISCUSSION AT THE NOBEL CONFERENCE

organized by Gustavus Adolphus College, St. Peter, Minnesota, 1971

edited by

JOHN D. ROSLANSKY

Woods Hole, Massachusetts

1972

NORTH-HOLLAND PUBLISHING COMPANY–AMSTERDAM · LONDON
FLEET ACADEMIC EDITIONS, INC.–NEW YORK

Library of Congress Catalog Card Number: 73–184999
ISBN North-Holland: 7204 4096 3

Publishers:

NORTH-HOLLAND PUBLISHING COMPANY — AMSTERDAM
NORTH-HOLLAND PUBLISHING COMPANY, LTD. — LONDON

Sole distributors for U.S.A. and Canada:
Fleet Academic Editions, Inc.
156 Fifth Avenue, New York, N.Y. 10010

PRINTED IN THE NETHERLANDS

Previous Nobel Conference volumes

Genetics and the Future of Man
The Control of Environment
The Human Mind
The Uniqueness of Man
Communication
Creativity

Editor's Acknowledgement

The 1971 Nobel Conference, assigned the topic, 'Shaping the Future', began with the fitting ceremony in which Norman E. Borlaug was awarded an honorary doctor's degree, the 30th Nobel Laureate to receive the award from Gustavus Adolphus College. It was appropriate since Dr. Borlaug's formative years had been spent on a northern Iowa farm, a mere one hundred miles from the campus.

Once again members of the greater college family, President and Mrs. Frank R. Barth, friends and associates, hosted the conference in a most magnanimous manner. Together with the distinguished group of futurist thinkers, a deadly serious effort ensued to probe rationally our future individually and collectively.

The Nobel Conference series started in 1965 through the initial support of the Hill Family Foundation. In subsequent years the Arnold Ryder Foundation, Tozer Foundation, Bremer Foundation and the Board of Education and Church Vocations of the Lutheran Church of America have been largely responsible for the continued support of the conference.

It is particularly fitting that this volume has been dedicated to Peyton Rous at the recommendation of Rockefeller University's Edward L. Tatum, who was kind enough to prepare his comments after consulting with Mrs. Rous.

Expression of gratitude for helpful discourse during preparation of the manuscripts must include many. It is especially appropriate to acknowledge discussions with May G. Wilson, Cornell University Medical School and Wallace O. Fenn, University of Rochester School of Medicine and Dentistry. Their deaths occurred prior to the publication of this volume on Shaping the Future, but their common sense reflections significantly contributed to shaping the future of many.

JOHN D. ROSLANSKY

Tribute to Peyton Rous
1879-1970

It seems eminently appropriate to dedicate this volume of the 1971 Nobel Conference, 'Shaping the Future', to Peyton Rous. Throughout his long and productive research career in biology and medicine, Rous did perhaps more towards shaping the future biological welfare and health of mankind than most individuals are privileged to do.

His now most widely recognized and best known discovery established for the first time the role of a virus as the causal agent of an animal tumor. This research, in 1911, so far anticipated other discoveries yet to be made that it was questioned, doubted, or largely ignored for many years. However, work over the following several decades, stimulated by his findings, and facilitated by the development of new techniques and biological materials, amply confirmed and expanded his results. The wide acceptance of his basic concepts of cancer led in 1966 to his Nobel Award in Physiology or Medicine. His work in this field may rightly be judged to have been one of the major milestones in the present rapid progress towards the understanding and future conquest of cancer.

Peyton Rous' research contributions to man's health were by no means limited to the field of cancer, but included studies which made possible the practical storage and use of human blood and blood fractions in transfusions, and important work on gall bladder function and on liver regeneration.

In appraising Rous' overall place in medical research, however, another aspect of his influence must be given high ranking. This was his uncompromising insistence on scientific objectivity, high quality research and precise and unambiguous planning analysis and writing. As Editor of the Journal of Experimental Medicine for approximately 50 years, and for 60 years as a member of the Rockefeller Institute, later the Rockefeller University, he inspired all with whom he had any contact, by his unflagging and generous example and guidance.

With all these attributes and contributions it is perhaps as a warm human being, with wide intellectual interests not only in science, but also in literature and the humanities, that he is best remembered by his many friends and associates.

Peyton Rous, in his life and contributions, by example and influence, thus may justly be said to have done more than most in helping to shape the future of mankind. It is with these thoughts in mind that this volume is dedicated to him.

EDWARD L. TATUM
The Rockefeller University

Contents

JOHN McHALE

Shaping the future:
Problems, priorities and imperatives

DR. JOHN McHALE *is the director of the Center for Integrative Studies, School of Advanced Technology, at the State University of New York, Binghamton.*

He holds a Ph. D. in sociology and is also an artist and writer, having published extensively in the United States and in Europe.

Dr. McHale is a Fellow of the World Academy of Art and Science and of the Royal Society of Arts in England. He has been awarded the Medaille D'Honneur en Vermeil, by the Société d'Encouragement au Progrès in France.

A noted lecturer and instructor, he has spoken and taught at various institutions in England and the United States.

His papers and articles about the impact of technology on culture, mass communications, and the future, have been published in the magazines The Futurist, American Behavioral Scientist, Futures Journal, Architectural Design, Ekistics *and* Current Magazine.

Dr. McHale has produced films and television shows dealing with city planning, ecology, and world population.

The Futurist *said his first book,* The Future of the Future, *was 'a good book to recommend to newcomers (to the study of the future).' His latest book is* The Ecological Context.

The idea that we may directly influence and positively shape our future(s) both individually and collectively, is relatively new in human experience. People have always been preoccupied, in one way or another, with *predicting* the future – but the capacity to shape actively any chosen future outcome was, for the greater part of human history, severely limited – by the meager control over the forces which molded human existence.

Life was relatively short, the resources to sustain life were usually scarce, hard-won, and inequably distributed. For most people and previous societies, the future was largely a continuation of the past beyond a relatively unchanging and unchangeable present. The larger realities were birth and death which bounded the unknown; the remote future was unknowable – and, to an extent unthinkable.

The emergence of our Western view of the future, therefore, has been historically unique in several regards:

(i) It embodies within it *the idea of progress*, where many earlier societies operated on cyclical models of change in which futures were variously predestined or returned upon the present and the past, upon their myths of origin.

(ii) As an idea, it is both *material* and *metaphysical*. It contains within it the notion of the material control and physical improvement of factors governing individual and collective welfare. It is metaphysical in its striving towards some degree of perfectibility of human institutions, of man and his society.

Thinking about the future remains, therefore, an idealistic and utopian enterprise. It assumes its specifically unique character, however, in a period when the material means become available, for the first time, on a scale which matches up to the idealism.

This potential degree of material control – both positive and negative – which we may now exercise in determining our future is quite unprecedented in all human experience.

This contemporary sense of the future, with its feeling of imminence and urgency, has been engendered by our exposure in a very brief period to the greatest acceleration of change in human history. In just over one hundred years – roughly three generations – we have had a series of successive technological, scientific, social and economic revolutions pressing ever more closely one upon the other. Historically accustomed to little or no apparent change, to geographic remoteness and relatively isolated local autonomy, we have suddenly been thrust into a complexly interdependent global community, in which change has become the norm, and in which the repercussions of any major event affecting any part of that community are swiftly felt throughout the world.

The crucial aspect of this evolutionary transition is that it marks the stage of emergence of human activities at magnitudes capable of large-scale and long-term interference with the overall ecological balance of planetary life.

For example:

(a) In the explosive growth of human population alone, this represents one of the largest biological upheavals in historical as well as geological time.

(b) In the transformation of the planet to human use, we have now pushed our frontiers
   – vertically into the air, to travel above the earth's surface and beyond its atmosphere.

- below the surface of the land, to extract and consume more energy and materials in this brief period than in all history.
- downward into the oceans to exploit more fully its food, mineral and other resources.

We now deal in radioactive, electronic, sonic and other energies which expand our controlled manipulation of our environment into hitherto unknown ranges of the electromagnetic spectrum. Astronomical amounts of goods may be produced with fractional inputs of human and machine energies, so that we have gone from marginal survival to potential abundance for all in three generations. This ongoing revolution has, in effect, changed almost all the ground rules which have governed the human condition.

From this time on, all major elements of the human enterprise are now seen to be closely interlocked in a 'man-made' ecosystem which has to be considered as an integral 'organic' sector of the earth's ecology. The range and magnitude of our technological intrusions into the planetary biosphere are now such that all of our large scale techno-industrial undertakings need, increasingly, to be gauged in terms of their long range consequences and implications for the global community.

In similar fashion, the scale of many of our global technological systems (i.e. of production, distribution, transportation and communications) has gone beyond the capacities of any single nation or group of nations to sustain and wholly operate. They require, and are dependent upon, the resource range of the entire earth for the metals and materials of which they are built and the energies to run them – in which no single nation is now self sufficient. The whole planetary life-support system increasingly relies upon the global interchange not only of physical resources and finished products, but of the knowledge pool of research, development, technical and managerial expertise, and the highly trained personnel who sustain and expand this.

In these combined senses, and at this scale, there are few 'wholly' local problems anymore, such as may be left entirely to the short range economic, expediency or temporary ideological preference of some exclusively national concerns. Many of the decisions affecting the disposition, use and operation of our large scale technologies go far beyond the relatively brief commercial, economic or political mandates of local decision making. Air, water and soil pollution are not local – the air is not restrained within municipal or national boundaries, nor are the oceans.

We have reached the point in human affairs at which the major socio-ecological requirements for sustaining the world community may take precedence over, and be superogative to, the more transient value systems and vested interests of any specific society.

When we consider, therefore, how we may *shape our future*, the problems, priorities and imperatives must be set within this new global reality. Firstly, let us consider the problems. In terms of problem definition and priorities, the continued disparities between the so-called advanced nations and the lesser developed may be viewed as the gravest threat in our immediate future. The explosive rises in population, the pressures on food lands and other resources, the scale of human wastage, environmental destruction, and the social disorganisation and pestilence accompanying even our limited wars are also linked in due measure to the revolutions in human expectations which now circle the globe.

These disparities between the *haves* and the *have nots* may also be defined as part of a growing ecological imbalance in which the 'hyperactive' advanced economies extract, produce and consume more, with more waste by-products, than the lesser developed, and by their increased dependence on raw materials from the latter now exist in a directly parasitic relationship to them.

In terms of energy use, the more fortunate individual in the industrial countries consumes more than fifty times that of his counterpart in the poorer regions, and contributes in due measure much more than fifty times the by-product pollutants now critically affecting the global environ systems.

Overall the advanced countries in the past decade consumed:

> 77% of all the coal
> 81% of the petroleum
> 95% of the natural gas

for less than one quarter of the world's population – with one nation alone, the U.S.A., specifically using one third of the world's total industrial energy, and consuming approximately 40 per cent of the world's output of raw materials. In round terms, approximately 20 per cent of the world's population enjoys 80 per cent of the world's income – using more than half of all the earth's resources and producing a concomitant balance of the biospheric pollutants which now threaten the viability of the planet.

This gap between rich and poor has other salient features which make it one of the most critical problems facing man in the next decade. Present world population totals roughly 3.6 billion. With the current rate of increase, this will double to over 7 billion by the year 2000, in just 30 years. Over 80 per cent of that increase in people will be in those world regions which now face critical inadequacies – in Asia, Africa, and Latin America. This doubling of population in one generation means not only a necessary doubling in food supply but – if other relatively low material standards are to be maintained as well – it will require a doubling and tripling of housing, of city sizes, highways, consumer goods, etc. With equivalent expansion of industrial materials, extraction, production, and distribution which in turn will necessitate more than tripling the energy consumption of various fuels and so on.

In terms of our current environmental practices and present socio-economic and industrial organisation, the by-product pollution and deterioration of the world environment could be near catastrophe.

Though much attention is given to 'closing the gap' between rich and poor nations in traditional terms, through foreign aid, favorable trade balances, etc., it is rather more sobering to consider what this means in material terms. To bring the total world population up to the standard of Western material consumption would require, for example, more than 5 times the present world consumption of metals and minerals – which we could not do in terms of current industrial practices. The energy required for such living standards increase alone will be overwhelming.

Projecting such requirements for a future world population of 5 billion living at present U.S. levels, one analyst suggests that this:

> 'would require 25 times as much energy as the U.S. does today ... (and) at 25 times the present U.S. consumption of coal, oil, and gas, the human race would burn up the earth's estimated reserves of fossil fuels not in a matter of centuries but in a few decades.'[1]

Energy and materials are not the whole story ... but water supply, health, literacy, housing and general human welfare.

---

[1] *Population Bulletin* No. 2, Vol. XXVI, 1970, Population Reference Bureau, Inc., Washington, D.C.

Despite all of the excellent work of the U.N. and its agencies of the 'green revolution' and other magnificent efforts, we are still not gaining rapidly enough to close the gap between the rich and poor nations. And critical though this is, it is only one facet of the overall world problem. Even where we refer to the *so-called advanced* nations as enjoying higher material standards of living, the quality of life in such societies is also in question where they are already faced with severe dislocation, deterioration, and obsolescence in critical areas of their socio-economic and political structures. Many of their internal institutions are archaic, strained towards breakdown and their physical environs are still suffering from the backlash of the developmental phases of unrestrained and unplanned economic and industrial exploitation.

Whilst evincing apprehension about the future and paying much lip service to change, even most of the advanced nations are reluctant to free themselves from the past. Though we refer so glibly to such advanced scientific and technological societies, no one of these yet has approached the beginnings of what might be termed a scientific society (i.e. one whose motivations, goals and orientations are permeated with the scientific outlook in the larger sense).

We should underline here that in terms of future options and alternatives, the solution(s) to our most critical world problems are indeed well within our developing scientific and technological capabilities – but it will require a more massive undertaking than is presently evident in our pious hopes and reliance on traditional practices. For example, our global defence establishments currently encompass a very large fraction of the highest scientific and technical expertise available in the world. Present outlays for military purposes total almost 10 per cent of the world's annual output of goods and services; over 50 million people are presently occupied with the maintenance of the networks of armed forces, bases, communication services, research, development and production facilities. One of the greatest priorities which now faces us is how we may turn such negative forces to positive advantage – to apply our cooperative energies to those human problems which threaten the very survival of our societies.

Wholly political and ideological approaches are now patently bankrupt. Conventional politics is no longer the art of the possible, it is now more a device for obscuring and avoiding the inevitable. At a time when organised knowledge allows us to accomplish the most audacious of yesterday's impossibles, the so-called expediencies and realities of the conventional political and economic wisdom are dangerously outmoded. The key to many of our present dilemmas lies in the identification of those social orientations which had great survival value in the past, but which now endanger our survival in the present and cripple our approach to the future.

We should emphasise here that no mere cataloguing of scientific developments, and technological possibilities or forecast of possibly impending options and alternatives will suffice to render the form of our emerging futures. It is not these external forces and impending crises which, in the end, shape our futures. Their occurrence, consequences and implications lie more than ever before within human control and decision.

Our core concern, therefore, should be with:

(i)   the necessary changes in values, attitudes, and motivations which determine how we now use our developed capabilities.

(ii) a massive reformulation of our goals and objectives.

(iii) the recognition that our future(s) are now shaped not only by what is possible or probable, but by what we deem to be desirable in human terms.

The approach towards considering and planning such humanly desirable futures lies via a further series of conceptual, economic, and social revolutions – in which the form of society itself must be reconceptualised and recast. We are all poised in the transition from the 'old' world to the new – literally on the hinge of the greatest evolutionary transformation in the human condition. In many cases, therefore, much of what we now perceive as manifestation of chaos and disorder is indeed the struggle towards emergence of newly evolving forms of order.

When we turn to questions of conscious 'ethical' control of our developed capacities on the planetary scale, our historical experience may be of little value. The socio-ethical attitudes which manifestly controlled the development of most pre-industrial societies and all early industrialising societies in the West, were largely based on marginal and competitive survival. Resources were limited, inequably distributed and access to them lay mainly through the exercise of physical power or other coercive means. Individuals, institutions, and communities were considered as relatively autonomous and self sufficient. Their survival was predicated on the freedom and ingenuity with which they modified and exploited the social and physical environment to their self-determined ends. Ethical values in such societies tended to confirm the prevailing survival mode and to be constrained within its limited possibilities for choice and action. Questions regarding the quality of human life, and of the environment, were relegated to individual concern, measured within the short range criteria of institutional and commercial needs, or subsumed under the prior requirements of national security.

The questions we now need to ask about man's relation to his world cannot be phrased without the knowledge that man makes himself – or he is not made at all! Humanity and its evolving destiny is, in this sense, superogative to any system devised by man. Relieved of the earlier survival pressures which forced social cohesion on the basis of a necessarily collective uniformity of directions, many alternate modes of individual and group directions and life styles become feasible. The tolerance of individual deviance of various kinds no longer threatening to the survival of society becomes not only possible, but probably necessary, to ensure the range of evolutionary diversity.

The models of human society, of our institutions, and of our social capabilities with which we still operate, tend to restrict much of our thinking within obsolete historical conditions. Much of our malaise and the widespread feeling of a 'world out of control' arises from the inadequacy of our traditional institutions, attitudes and values. These were, in the main, formed in other periods, in conditions of marginal survival and economies of scarcity whose constraining premises are no longer relevant. Faced with potential abundance, they are productive of unease and insecurity; confronted with freedom, they will often assume new forms of slavery.

When many of our societies can produce material goods far beyond immediate necessity, and have elaborated their organisational capabilities far beyond those necessary for mere group survival and security, our outdated socio-economic and political models still generate the same sets of 'dilemma' and 'crisis' responses to most of our problems. The constraining myths and values that bind us to obsolete forms, old fears, and insecurities may be our most dangerous 'deterrents' in the modern world. Our traditional ideologies are inadequate guides to the future, serving mainly to perpetuate old inequities and rivalries and through them to create new wars and tensions. The full significance of our newly evolving scientific, social, and industrial capabilities is still barely understood –

even by those who have invented their components, organised their productive capacities and are responsible for their expansion. Their basic implications run counter to almost every past survival strategy which we have so painfully accumulated.

Our present generation now faces the future with globally developed physical capabilities which may free man for the first time in history, from the age old 'fear' constraints of material scarcity, individual and group insecurity and competition for life survival through access to limited resources. At this point in the mid 20th century, the large scale development of scientific and technological means has changed almost all of the socio-ethical 'ground rules' upon which human society has previously operated. The use of such means has not only created a new kind of reality, but permits the coexistence, and choice, of many different 'realities'.

Socio-ethical decisions regarding the human condition need no longer be phrased in terms of what we *can* do, but in terms of what we *choose* to do, both individually and collectively. Such choices, in terms of the conscious control of what has hitherto been a largely unconscious and locally controlled enterprise, will require a radical reconceptualisation of the degree to which man chooses individually and the ways in which these individual choices are subsumed within the larger evolutionary pattern. In this sense, our most urgent imperatives are now non-technological in the physical sense. The future of human society is less centrally dependent on further technological elaboration, but rather more on developing the socially innovative means to use our technological capacities. As we have consciously learnt in the past few decades how to organise scientific and technical development on the largest scale, so now we must orient ourselves to the conscious process of *social invention*, to the remolding and reshaping of our institutions, organisations and value systems. No mandate exists at the world level to shape our futures. No single nation, or international agency has the power, resource, and capabilities to assume such a mandate.

The new 'polity' is the world community. The forward conduct of that polity now requires the assumption of new individual and collective initiatives – self-organised and self-coordinated on a global scale. This will need what H. G. Wells termed 'the Open Conspiracy', through which individuals and groups may deliberately seek ways around, and over, the various social, political and ideological 'roadblocks' which now threaten our global survival.

Our basic questions in shaping our future now revolve around the overall socio-ecological maintenance of our emerging planetary society. What are the optimal conditions for human society on earth? There is obviously no fixed answer to such a question. But there are the various physical factors of adequacy in food, shelter, health, general welfare, and the concomitant access to the individually preferred physical and social facilities that make life meaningful and enjoyable. We have gradually arrived at sets of such conditions, as in the various bills of human rights, like that of the United Nations.

Whether such 'ground rules' may be practical or not, we do in effect approach them, however tentatively, when we try to legislate for some human-welfare or environmental-control measure. The time is now overdue for much more than tentative or local measures. To design our way forward through our present critical transitions, we need to adopt some more positive and operational indicators of the optimal conditions for the fulfillment of human life. By this, we do not mean optimal determinants that may be valid for all time and all people, that is, some set of absolutes. The variable and changing nature of human values makes this not only undesirable but unrealistic, in that one set of values in development may considerably modify others. But such considerations may still be flexibly accommodated and yet allow adequate definition.

We may tackle this in other ways by asking various fundamental questions about our planetary society. Which activities are most inimical to this; which more positively sustain, and forward, the human enterprise?

What are *the physical limits and constraints in the overall ecosystem*, with regard to our growing technological systems?

What are *the relevant human limits*, for example, the biological limits; air, food, water, temperature, space, speed, and noise tolerances?

What are *the irreplaceable resource limits*, for example, both the physical energy and material resources, and the human individual, social, and genetic resources?

The core of our discussion has revolved around the same inquiry, repeated in different ways:

What are the socio-physical operational parameters for the planet – the ecological or housekeeping rules that must now govern human occupancy? These are very large questions, but they are those to which we must now apply ourselves – in many different ways and over a very long period. Some of the answers we already know, in part. Others are, in some senses, ultimately unanswerable. That they may be so is the more reason to ask them, if only to probe the limits of our knowledge.

The way towards the future lies neither with a corrosive pessimism that we are in a 'runaway world' nor with the equally evasive optimism that we may continue to muddle through with 'business as usual'. It requires rather a renewed reconceptualisation of man himself, of his ideas and beliefs, and of the recognition that he is now in charge of his own destiny.

NORMAN E. BORLAUG

The world food problem –
present and future

DR. NORMAN E. BORLAUG *has recently returned from Oslo, Norway, where he received the Nobel Prize for Peace during special ceremonies on December 10. He was awarded the Nobel Prize for literally saving millions from malnutrition and starvation through the development of a high-yielding dwarf variety of wheat.*

Dr. Borlaug was born in Cresco, Iowa, in 1914. His college career — from bachelor to Ph. D. — began and ended (1942) on the campus of the University of Minnesota.

From 1942 to 1944 he was a microbiologist with E. I. DuPont and Company in charge of research on industrial and agricultural bactericide, fungicide, and preservatives. In 1944, as a Geneticist and Plant Pathologist, he organized and directed the Cooperative Wheat Research and Production Program in Mexico. This program was sponsored jointly by the Mexican Government and the Rockefeller Foundation.

Since 1962 he has been Director of the Wheat Program of the International Center for Maize and Wheat Improvement. During this period, Dr. Borlaug has devoted most of his efforts to wheat research and production problems, and to the training of young wheat scientists on a global basis. He also has devoted a large part of his effort to assisting programs in six Latin American countries and in eight Near and Middle East countries, including Pakistan and India. More than 140 young scientists from these countries have been trained in Mexico under his direction.

Dr. Borlaug has been the recipient of over 20 citations and awards from universities, countries, cities, and organizations throughout the world.

The scope and magnitude of the problems that confront the human race during these next few decades are very complex, I feel this to the very bottom of my feet. I have worked largely on only one aspect of this complex problem and I would like to give you a little background so you will understand some of my remarks:

I was born on a very small farm very close to this part of Minnesota, just across into northeast Iowa and this gave me a good background of experience from which to begin a lifetime profession on food production. I can understand the socio-economic problems of the small farmer and I can communicate rather well sometimes even without being able to do so through language. This has been most helpful to me. I came up through simple beginnings, a one room country school. My original work at the University of Minnesota was not in agriculture or plant breeding in the narrow context, but in forestry in its broadest aspects: the ecology and silvics of our forest, our watersheds, and our wildlife and water, so I am sensitive to many of these other human needs beyond the one of immediate food.

Now I would like to tell you a little about what the situation is on food to lead off, and then how I react to this very complex problem that confronts the young people of your generation, and that will confront the generation of your children.

It's a sad tragedy that, despite the very privileged people of the United States and a few other countries where food exists in abundance, there still exists the problem of distributing this food to some of our underprivileged people. I am sure that we are making some progress at correcting this, but more is needed to provide that unfortunate segment of society with this very basic commodity. The United Nations Food and Agricultural Organization estimates that more than half of the people of this planet are hungry at least several times during the course of a week and more than that half, even worse, are malnourished, short especially of proteins which affect their whole development, both physical and mental. It's becoming more and more clear as more evidence is accumulated by our medical scientists and nutritionists that the tragedy is not restricted to those who die from starvation, but even worse, those who are malnourished in early infancy, but who survive often have been damaged in mental capacity for the rest of their life. Much of this malnutrition damage takes place from the time the baby is weaned through the first 2 to 5 years of growth. This is a very critical period and it is one that we are only now beginning to become concerned about. The whole emphasis in the past has been one of producing enough food and we could only give secondary attention to producing the right kind of food.

Now, if we have this kind of a situation in the world it's not a very pleasant world, despite the fact that from your vantage point it looks prosperous. What can we do about it? I have spent most of my professional career working in the hungry nations of the world trying in my own modest way to do something about improving the situation. Very modest has been the progress indeed, but in recent years there has been some hope. Changes have started to occur, the tide has changed, it has been labeled by the popular press as the Green Revolution but we can't become complacent. Shortage of food is a tremendous problem and a continuing problem. From what we have learned so far we have been able to buy for your generation maybe two or three decades of time in which to solve these problems, if we continue to push ahead aggressively.

Just what is involved in provoking change in a traditional agriculture? I should point out to you that agriculture here in the USA is a very efficient industry. Yet it has recently become the Ugly Duckling in our affluent urban society.

Five per cent of the people produce enough food for this country, plus very large quantities of food for export. Yet in the hungry nations anywhere from 70 to 80 per cent, or more, of the total population are engaged in a livelihood of subsistence agriculture, tied to a small piece of land, living under impoverished conditions, with even inadequate food despite all of their efforts. Not at all a pleasant picture. And what is worse, to provoke change in such a society is one of the most frustrating and difficult situations that you can encounter in this world, because these poverty stricken societies are in such a poor position to help themselves. Almost invariably there is a lack of trained people, beginning with school teachers at all levels and ending with scientists who can provoke the kind of technological and scientific change that may raise the standard of living. In India and Pakistan, two of the nations with extreme food shortages, we have recently drawn on our experience in Mexico which was in just such a situation twenty-six years ago when we began working there. We found through experience one must begin attacking these problems of increased food production by establishing a research program, not working on narrow disciplines but on all of those inter-related factors that must be integrated to produce a final effect to increase production. In the developing countries it is not the number of profound scientific treatises or publications that appear in scientific journals that will help to make changes. Change must be measured by the increase in tons of grain be it wheat, rice, corn, sorghum or millet; this must be your criterion of change, not the over-sophisticated approach, which we, the developed nations, have unfortunately sponsored in our university staff advancement philosophy of 'publish or perish'. Now, it takes a long time to train a generation of scientists. The schools and universities in the developing countries aren't functioning right; they aren't providing the right opportunities for the right kinds of people. Of those that do graduate, it takes time to find out which are really well motivated. I wouldn't give a nickel for the most talented scientist in the world or have him join my scientific team that works internationally, if he doesn't have social motivation and isn't interested in trying to help the people of the country to which he is assigned. I am not interested in those people who are only interested in their own personal ego and their advancement in their own special field. This won't help solve the big human problems that we face around the world. In a country where there are few or no trained people, it takes fifteen to eighteen years to develop a whole corps of scientists and teachers in adequate numbers to cope with this problem. The world food production problems are of such magnitude that we have to find shortcuts, we can't wait. We have to draw on certain international institutions such as the one that I have been affiliated with. The International Center for Maize and Wheat Improvement evolved from a country program, financed in part by the Mexican government and the Rockefeller Foundation, which within the last eight years has grown into an international research institute that has now much broader responsibilities, working not only in one country, but working in many hungry countries trying to provoke change. It took us ten years to solve Mexico's wheat production problem, working diligently and I hope creatively, but the magnitude of the problems that we began to face ten years later, when we began working in India and Pakistan, were of a very much greater scope. We analyzed the situation and decided we could not wait fifteen or eighteen years for results, we couldn't gradually train people as we did before in Mexico, there was no chance for a long period of gestation before we could get a result. The crisis was too urgent. We decided to bring many young scientists to our Mexico base and give them the best type of practical training that we were equipped to do. The same was done at the International Rice Institute in the Philippines where they were carrying out similar work on that important crop. Our approach is to make science function to serve human needs. It's quite a different approach from that of many very sophisticated academic institutions in the U.S.A. and Western Europe. We have an urgency, we live and work close to poverty, we know the tremendous need for rapid change. We try to inculcate this spirit of urgency into these young scientists and at the same time we try to train them in all of the disciplines that bear on food production. By this I mean genetics and its application in plant breeding to produce the new kinds of seeds which have an entirely different production potential when they are properly cultivated. We have to find out how to grow these new kinds of plants right: what kind of fertilizer, what kind of insect control, when to plant, how much to plant, how to conserve the moisture or how to apply it if it is irrigated. All of these are factors that are involved in changing production. And if you can bring them all to bear, sometimes you can make very spectacular changes in a very short time.

I say 'if' because you must simultaneously treat with two other very important groups of factors that I call the 'economic and physiologic factors'. You must insist that government economic policy is such that this small farmer, who has always been accused of being ultra-conservative to the point that he is unknown to change, will adopt the new. He has farmed the same way all his life, as had his father before him and his grandfather, back for generations and generations. He has been accused of being immutable from the standpoint of provoking social change. This unjust accusation has frequently been made, unfortunately by very sophisticated scholars, not only from one country but from around the world. So you must remove the economic roadblocks before the peasant farmer can adopt the new technology that has been developed by research. Economic policy must make the production of more grain profitable to this small farmer so it's worth his while to adopt the new technology. If you can only demonstrate a change of 10 per cent, he will not take the chance; if you can demonstrate a yield difference of 100 or 200 per cent, he's ready, assuming that the government policy is right so that it will be profitable, that the prices for his product are stabilized at a reasonable level; and that fertilizers are available on time and at the right price and with credit to help him to purchase them. The new technology must be demonstrated as widely as possible on small farmers' plots throughout the country so that they see it with their own eyes. The farmer will not be receptive if he sees there demonstrations done at government experiment stations or in university experimental plots. He is not sure how much of the change in grain yield is attributable to science and new technology and how much is 'witchcraft', but if he sees it done on his land or his neighbour's land, there is quite a different point of view on the psychology of change.

I have had the good fortune of seeing this change take place in several different countries: first, after a long hard struggle, in Mexico; more recently in Pakistan and India. In the latter two countries the food deficits have been of tremendous magnitude in the last six or seven years and without a doubt millions of people would have starved to death in the 1966 and

1967 crises had it not been for the importation of vast quantities of grain from United States, Canada and Australia. The magnitude of the change in India and Pakistan in the last three harvests surprised even me. The rapidity of change surpassed my fondest hopes. In India I have seen wheat production jump from the so-called highest pre-Green Revolution base – the very favorable year of 1965 in which India produced a harvest of 12 million metric tons – to more than 20 million metric tons last year. In Pakistan the total production has essentially doubled in that same period of time. These are dramatic changes that the world thought were impossible to achieve in this short period of time. The most significant thing of all, as far as I'm concerned, has been to disprove that the small farmer, this small, peasant farmer, would not change. He'll change if you help him change. You have to help him at all levels; not only at the scientific but at the top government levels with proper government economic policy. This is not an easy task. When you train a group of new scientists and they move back in their old environment it's impossible for them to break through very often. You young people are so right; the top scientist is there because of seniority and he's all too often a fossil that 'hasn't been dug down yet'.

In the last seminar I always give these young scientists before they leave Mexico, I say, 'Don't be too impatient, too fast, or you will destroy yourself. You bring a new philosophy, a new approach to scientific problems. We want to provoke constructive change; let's not be destructive or in the process you will destroy yourself and whatever hope we have for provoking constructive change. Remember it is easy to destroy but very difficult to build constructively.' At the same time somebody from the outside must try to put an umbrella over these young people after they have returned home to protect them and to keep them working together as a team in so far as

is possible while simultaneously trying to convince government that they have to change policy on the price structure
and the availability of inputs as well as at the same time give
these young people a chance to use their talents. You don't accomplish this in 24 hours or in 24 months, but you can do a
surprising lot once you learn how to operate like a skilled
torero (bull-fighter) while avoiding getting your leg torn off;
because you yourself are also as vulnerable coming in from
the outside when dealing with the stratified, social government situation as the young student is who is returning to his
country. You must be deft, you must know how far you can
go and how fast or you will destroy any opportunity you have
for provoking constructive change.

In the process, in the heat of battle trying to accomplish
these changes I have often wondered and thought: Wouldn't
it be wonderful if a person were deaf and if he were blind and
if he had a skin and a hide as thick as that of a rhinoceros
through all of the accusations that are leveled at you? But you
must control yourself, you must go on, you must struggle,
and suddenly things will start improving if your science and
economics are right, and you will have the great satisfaction
of seeing constructive change.

I have talked about food, but the game is bigger than food
production. From wheat alone – while there is also a very
dramatic change in rice production and more recently in corn
in some of these countries – in the last three harvests the gross
national product in India has increased by a billion eight hundred million (1.8 billion) dollars. This is largely money that
has gone into the pockets of the small farmers. This vast segment of the society begins to enter into the economy of the
country for the first time. When the peasant farmer has money
he starts buying things that he was never able to buy before;
he had lived outside the economy. This starts a whole series

of changes. Some of them are good, most of them are good; some of them are not so good. He begins to buy simple little machines that make his farming more efficient. It doesn't necessarily displace people into the slums of the large cities if it's handled wisely. He begins to buy fertilizer and things that he has to have in order to increase his output. He begins to buy transistor radios and if the governments are wise, they can reach many villages that they have never reached with public schools. The ultimate success will depend on the government and its vision. Sewing machines come into the village, better transportation, the government begins to demand a school or better schools. There is a whole psychological change. Despair, which was widespread in India and Pakistan only five years ago, is being replaced by hope and a new enthusiasm.

Now, how do we keep this alive? With what we have now achieved we have bought a few years of time. If we can convince governments to allocate their resources wisely and if we can find and train the right young talent, in sufficient numbers, the right kind of people who want to become scientists and improve the lot of the poverty stricken masses of the world, we can continue to make progress.

There are an increasing number of new opportunities becoming available in international programs, but we need dedicated well-prepared people. It is not enough to be a political idealist, we need young people with scientific skills and training and the mental and physical toughness, discipline, and motivation to implement these skills for the improvement of the lot of mankind. There is altogether too much wishful thinking that empty words will fill empty bellies and solve the problems of the world. You can't build a better world on empty idealistic words alone. Cozy words do not change the type of government nor does a change of government solve automatically the basic problems of hunger and poverty. That solution would be wonderful and simple. But it isn't forth-coming. These same basic problems confront all govern-ments from the extreme left to the extreme right and all of those in the middle of the road in the developing countries. Working on food, I have had the unique pleasure and oppor-tunity of working with all types of governments in one capac-ity or the other. I have twice visited Algeria within the last year, looking at its agricultural problem, talking to its officials and trying to formulate some type of rational program, trying to outline for them some training program for their young scientists, who are practically non-existent. They had eleven university trained scientists in agriculture at the B.S. level when they gained their independence. Algeria is a vast coun-try. What do you do? We can't wait; we've got to start training at all levels. I was recently in Russia and I see the same prob-lems. They have somewhat different problems in that theirs are mainly problems of production. I think the communistic countries distribute what production they have better than we do, here in this country, but they are less efficient in produc-tion. I say that the United States with its vast food production must find a way to assure food to the underprivileged sectors of our society. I am not in a position to say how to do it. I say you have the wealth and the ability to do it if you have the will. And yet I must say that there are many confusing issues that can make this water very muddy. It's easy to level your finger at government and say that they have not taken action, but sometimes when they try to take action to improve the lot of these unfortunates through expanding, let's say, the Food Stamp Program, there are 'dropouts' that take advantage of this and this provokes a reaction again from government or certain sectors of government, and the whole issue is at stake. *You can't be a dropout in this kind of a society* – the world society of today. No matter what you do, without food you will only live three weeks, assuming you are starting with a good, vigorous body and a good healthy condition. And if you are ill or already poorly nourished, it will be much less than three weeks. And each and every day when you eat whatever it is, you owe somebody in your society something. The food you consume daily is produced by the sweat of the brow of some person in some part of the world. You haven't dropped out. I'm not talking to individuals; I am talking to the world in general. The easy way out is to 'drop out' and become a social parasite, a 'hippie'. But the world can't survive with too many of these social parasites who 'mouth empty idealistic slogans'.

All right, we have talked about trying to increase food production. We have made modest progress recently; I think that we can stay ahead, but we haven't solved it. We can stay ahead for two or three decades if we get the right support from all kinds of governments. It is very questionable that we will continue to do so unless we continue to fight more effectively than we have in the past. It's much easier to get big budgets for national defense even in the developing countries than it is for food production. So, you see, you don't solve these problems easily. You have to keep fighting, you have to keep struggling and you have to keep trying to stimulate the young scientists to work together in a team effort. If they each go their own way, they will be devoured by their environment and they will never be effective. Staying together and each biding his own time until he grows in stature and experience and advances in his own system, they will change the system and become more effective – but you don't do this overnight.

But food isn't enough. We look at how fast we are growing in human numbers and I'm sure it's the will and hope of every person in this audience that we can see the standard of living of all of the peoples of the world improve, especially of those unfortunates in the developing countries who are hungry and short of the other basic necessities of life. It isn't just food. What about employment opportunities? I am of the firm be-belief that the vast energies of youth with their strong bodies have a great deal to contribute. These energies must be burn-ed and utilized for good, for constructive programs, not for destructive purposes. Sometimes I think our whole social structure has gone too far in the direction of protecting our youth. We have over-reacted in trying to correct the abuses on child labor prior to the enactment of the child labor legis-lation. Now we have a situation where it is very difficult for young people to get jobs even during the summer vacation. Up to a point we have defeated our own purpose. I think we have to re-examine this whole issue. The tremendous ener-gy of youth will be used for good if it is given the opportuni-ty, or will be used destructively all too often if this opportu-nity is not provided.

Quite apart from employment, what about medical care? Look at the miserable nations of the world. Even here, in this country, in the slums it's not pleasant. What about ade-quate housing? Adequate clothing? Transportation? Recrea-tion? Most of the underprivileged people of the world don't even know what this word is. They are too busy struggling to exist. As we grow in human numbers and we pile up people in our own large cities, what about the strains and stresses and all of the unpleasantries that go with this, especially in the slums and in the ghettos? Are we doing enough to correct it? Do we even understand the problem that is involved? I doubt it very much. Looking at experimental animals there is a lot of evidence to be seen and yet there are those that say, 'Oh, you can't compare man to rat.' I say sometimes there is a great similarity between two legged rats and four legged rats. But in a serious vein, these experimental animals can tell us a great deal; maybe you have to make extrapolations to apply this to the human needs.

What happens when populations of rats grow too dense? They can't stand the stress and go beserk and their society collapses. What happens to the snowshoe hare here in Northern Minnesota and Wisconsin and Michigan and Manitoba, when populations become too dense? For thirty years their dying was misinterpreted as being from a shortage of food. It was not. Then a virus was looked for and never found. About 7 years ago it suddenly became evident from some studies in endocrinology that when snowshoe hares get too crowded, some cannot stand this condition and they just have internal hemorrhages and die.

The only difference between that snowshoe hare and a human being is that when we get all crowded up together, we go out and club one of our neighbors on the head but the old snowshoe hare just lies down and dies, peacefully. In our animal societies there are built in devices for controlling their numbers to fit in to the carrying capacity of the habitat or environment. It makes no difference whether you are talking about lions in the free in East Africa, the snowshoe hare here in Minnesota, or the Arctic lemming. The Arctic lemming is, of course, a suicidal species. His population builds up, he gets nervous, and it's unfortunate but true that the young of the population start migrating madly to the ocean and drown themselves in vast numbers. The small remaining part of the population again builds up.

All around about us we see these devices for population control in operation but they don't appear to exist in men. I am sure they do exist, but as social beings with our evolution and our concept of societies, we have tried to protect the life of each man and the result is that our numbers keep growing. If we aren't wise enough to adjust our population growth to the carrying capacity of our planet it will get to a point where we all starve to death or kill ourselves by beating each other on the head. Our own built-in-mechanisms would adjust, but would it be pleasant? Would it be pleasant to see these young-sters that we hold highly in value dying of starvation, of disease, of this or that? I don't think so. It's against the Christian ethic and so we have to come to grips with these problems.

Today everybody talks about environment and those that are talking about environment are talking about 15 different aspects of the environment. The total erosion or degradation of the environment is the interaction of all of the physical and biologic forces on this planet. And of those biological entities, the worst one is man, and the more and faster we grow in human numbers the more difficulties we are going to have. Now, there is no question but that we have been neglectful of coping with this. We have polluted streams and rivers and lakes. That pollution is in the ocean already. Per-haps the tuna have a lot of mercury content but the sad part is that in many cases we don't have good bench marks of what that content was before. We're dealing with levels that some-times we know very little about when it comes to both imme-diate and long term effects on human and other living species that inhabit the environment around us. We need to know more, but again this takes time, and you cannot say, we will im-mediately change this, because we must recognize that we are dealing with many imponderables that we have very little data for. For example, Maine said three years ago, we will use no more DDT. Perhaps a wise policy because of the effect it has in building up in certain of the food chains when used on for-ests and watershed areas. But, you will notice that last summer in order to save the forest from gypsy moth it was necessary to go back and use reasonable levels of DDT at critical times.

DDT – now widely damned – has saved the lives of millions from malaria. What this really means is that we have to weigh each case. I have had people say to me within the last few weeks, What about all this fertilizer? If you are advocating its use for the expansion of wheat production and rice production, in the developing countries, isn't this greatly adding to the deterioration of our environment by being leached into our streams and bodies of water? Well, I think this is a vast over-simplification when we are talking about nitrogen and also phosphate. And, it's one thing for the USA and all its privileged to speak this way when we enjoy an abundance of food. Perhaps if one were to put back into production all of the agricultural lands that have been taken out of production and you made a complete reversal back to organic farming with clovers, alfalfa, and soybeans as a crop rotation with corn, wheat and barley, you could perhaps produce the food and convert it into the necessary animal products, meat, milk and eggs sufficient for a period of 10 to 20 years. But that's not the solution necessarily. What will happen to the price of food? To achieve this the price would probably double, triple or maybe more than triple. What's going to happen to the low income people?

What is worse, well-fed privileged people from the developed countries, especially the USA, pose these simple solutions and say, 'Why are you advocating this sort of thing in India?' The only answer that I can think of is: Do you deny these people the chance to improve their standard of living, since the amount of land available per capita to them is already only one-fifth of what it is in this country? Do you say that it is morally incorrect to use chemical fertilizers under these conditions? Do you think you can build world peace on poverty, empty bellies and empty words? The man in India cannot make the change to legumes. I spent my first three years in

India talking down this fallacious approach of organic farming as a solution to food production problems. They can never make a breakthrough in production employing organic farming techniques where they are land hungry first and then cereal grain hungry.

So, again, *unless there is the right mixture of common sense and science and technology, the world is doomed.* The whole world wants simple answers. We all get imbued with the importance of our own discipline. I am very fearful that we are doing a most miserable job of communication between the social sciences and the biological and physical sciences as well as between many other disciplines in our society. I am very concerned about the criteria being used by the people who are passing judgment on human behavior. I am going to be blunt and to the point – this includes the lawyers and judges and, I am sorry to say, I must include many who serve on juries. They are passing judgment on the behavior of Homo Sapiens – a biological species. All too often decisions or verdicts are based on the false premise that all people are the same. In this room, with the possible exception of some identical twins who may be present, there are no two people that are identical in physical make up, in mental capacity, and in behavior under different stresses and stimuli. This is all lost track of when we go to interpretation of how we behave under our own system of laws; and it gets confused when we talk about the right of the individual and the right of the society. What is really often on trial is the trial of democracy, the democratic way of life. I have lived and worked in governments from the extreme left to the extremely militaristic ones on the right and I prefer the middle of the road, the democracy. But in order to keep democracy alive we must understand that there are certain rights of society that up to a point cannot be infringed on without bringing down in ruin that society, that democratic society.

Twenty years ago I saw Uruguay held up as the model of democracy in Latin America, the Switzerland of Latin America. Look at its seething pain and agony today; inflationists destroyed its viability; dissension and chaos rule the land. I saw Chile, with the most advanced social legislation in Latin America before the last war, have its economy eroded away, again by inflation. It wouldn't come to grips with this; it slid into a different kind of democracy, into a social democracy. I do not here intend to discuss the pros and cons of one or the other; I am simply stating bluntly and boldly that I want the middle of the road where I hang my hat. I think if all of us weighed all of these values with which we have been blessed we, too, will decide that the middle of the way is the most humane way. You can throw the 'scoundrels' out with the ballot in a democracy but you have lost this prerogative with extreme governments of either the right or left.

Now, all of these aspects of human needs become a nine-headed monster with the longest, most menacing tentacle that of population growth, that threatens to destroy us all as a world society. I am of the firm belief that we can no longer blindly go ahead, any more than many other countries have tried to do, and have an aristocracy or an elite protectively isolated from the poverty and misery of a vast segment of our society. That will not prevail for very long. It will be another Chile or another Cuba or another Russia. But neither can you have this kind of difference in standard of living in the world and have it exist very much longer. The world gets more crowded and whether or not we like to recognize or admit it, it is becoming more one world as Wendell Willkie long ago predicted. We need to understand the problems of our fellow man, not only within the country, but between different parts of the world. We need to have our democracy conditioned by the right blend of idealism and of science and technology that can give not only us, but all of the developing nations of the world a better standard of living. We have seen the consequences of trying to build a Utopia in the past. Plato tried it; he didn't succeed. Are we any smarter? I think that all too often we fail to read history from a critical point of view and learn from it. We point out all of the bad things that were done in the past. There are many lessons in history if we will approach it with an open mind. And to you youth I say, prepare yourself for building this better world; it will be your world very soon, and with it go all of the responsibilities. Prepare yourself with skills, not just with words and ideas. It's easy to criticize and destroy; it's very difficult indeed to build constructively. And, again, don't look for easy solutions. They won't be forthcoming.

I would just like to bring home to you what the magnitude of this population problem is and how this population monster relates to all of these nine aspects. Each tick of the clock at the present time adds 2.2 additional people to the world's population that must be given some semblance of a decent life, and this means that each year we add to the total world population 70 million mouths and stomachs and bodies. By 1980 it will go up to 2.7 per tick of the clock, and by 1990 it will be 3.3 and by the year 2000, and most of you young people are going to be here to see this change, the tick will be menacing louder and louder at the rate of 4 per second, with an increase of 125 million per year in 2000, unless we come to grips with this problem. Do we have the will? Do we have the desire? Unless we think and ponder this, I seriously doubt we will build a better world, and yet we can. We need idealists to build a better world, but to students and youth, I would repeat, don't be a dropout. You can't build a better world being a dropout. I have already pointed out that you automatically become a social parasite and the world has got too many of these. You young students know who the fakers and the demagogues are and who are the true idealists in your own student bodies. Fakers and demagogues exist in all segments of our society in all parts of the world in all age groups. We have ours in science and I am not proud to claim these as colleagues. Protect the democratic way of life. Identify these people for what they are or our democratic process will be doomed and short lived. And in order to produce a better world I don't think you need to be turned on with drugs. That's the weakling 'easy way out'. Don't get hooked. All of the energies that you have and the strong, good bodies that you have and the excellent minds, use them constructively. I don't need to be motivated by drugs. I went through the depression and I gained my education working for it. I have never regretted it. I carry no psychological or social callouses or scars of any kind despite my humble beginning. I'm proud of that simple heritage. At that time I enjoyed it. I reflect on it now with even greater joy and satisfaction. The world isn't worse now than it was in the depths of the depression in the 1930's. I have lived and looked at the standards of living in many parts of the world. It isn't as bad in the USA as we make it. There is plenty of hope and it's up to you, the youth of the USA, to make it better, not only for the USA, but for the rest of the world, and I am sure you will.

I'd like to point out that there are still some old people with good philosophy. I am sure most of you know Will Durant, the philosopher who wrote the Story of Philosophy. He and his wife, I suppose they are 85 years young, are now finishing writing a series of volumes on the Story of Mankind from the beginning of recorded history up to the present time. He is quoted in the August 13, 1965 issue of Time – he was then 79 years old, or young – as saying: 'In my youth I stressed freedom and in my old age I stress order. I have made the great discovery that liberty or freedom is a product of order. Sixty years ago when I was 19, I knew everything. Now I know nothing. I have made the great discovery that education is a progressive discovery of our own ignorance.'

ANTHONY J. WIENER

Faust's progress:
Methodology for
shaping the
future

DR. ANTHONY J. WIENER *is an analyst of public policy issues, and is especially interested in those involving social and political aspects of science and technology. In addition to participating in the management of Hudson Institute's research program, he has conducted studies and written reports on a range of public policy issues including the future of U.S. poverty, race relations and urban problems, arms control, international crises, and prospects for multinational business enterprises.*

Born in 1930, Dr. Wiener received the A.B. from Harvard University in 1952 and the J.D. from Harvard Law School in 1956. He joined Hudson Institute at its founding in 1961 and is now Chairman of the Research Management Council.

Prior to joining Hudson Institute, Dr. Wiener was associated with Arthur D. Little, Inc., where he was a consultant on political and economic aspects of science and technology. Earlier, he taught Science and Government and other political science courses at the Massachusetts Institute of Technology. As Research Staff Member of the Center for International Studies at M.I.T. he co-authored a study for the National Science Foundation on the social organization of science and technology in the U.S.S.R.

In 1969 he served as Chairman of the White House Urban Affairs Research Committee, and in 1970 as consultant to the President's National Goals Research Staff. He is a member of the Research Advisory Committee of the U.S. Educational Policy Research Center at Syracuse University, and Adjunct Professor of System Analysis and Public Policy at the Polytechnic Institute of Brooklyn.

Dr. Wiener's publications include The Year 2000: A Framework for Speculation, *in collaboration with Herman Kahn. He has been a lecturer at many universities and professional meetings and is a regular faculty member at executive seminars conducted by business schools, professional and managerial associations, and major corporations.*

How does one know anything about the future, let alone 'shape' it? How one knows something is very closely related to what it is he thinks he knows. And this is especially true of the future, because it doesn't exist. It is, at any given moment, only what people imagine. It doesn't exist because it hasn't happened yet. Many of the things that will actually happen and that will be very important don't belong to any distribution of probabilities we know anything about. They can't be described adequately in terms of a 'system', some heroic or foolish attempts to the contrary notwithstanding, since we don't know enough about the relevant system. We simply cannot know with any precision what's going to happen, even when it comes to very important concerns of ours. Therefore our hopes and fears come into play and often dominate our expectations.

Not long ago I talked with a college student who told me she had watched a television soap opera called 'Search for Tomorrow'. She said, 'I don't get it; why should anyone want to search for tomorrow? All you have to do is wait, and it'll come and get you.' This is one possible attitude toward the future; one that has recently become prevalent. There is a new pessimism, a feeling that the system doesn't work, that the future is full of problems worse than those people have faced in the past. There are some good reasons for feeling this way, but the feeling exists much more than objective reasons can account for.

We live in a society that has become unwilling to take credit for its successes. For example, the Green Revolution, to which Dr. Borlaug contributed so much, is an extraordinarily dramatic success, which opens the possibility of reversing what otherwise would have seemed an almost hopeless situation – the poverty trap of the underdeveloped countries, where it is impossible to accumulate any surplus over bare subsistence. For the first time it looks as though these countries, for a generation's time, or two or three at most, will have the opportunity to accumulate some wealth and to move beyond subsistence agriculture. They can make permanent their escape from poverty, by means of this opportunity, if at the same time they can learn to control their population growth. In this opportunity the world has an extraordinary success, which it refuses to acknowledge. The alternative, which but for the Green Revolution would have been almost certain, would have been a dismal, Malthusian series of famines.

In appraising the state of the society, in viewing what the future holds in store, it is characteristic of most people who think about these issues to be pessimistic and to fail to notice the ways in which our cup is at least partly full, if not running over. In fact, by almost any objective criterion, in contrast to subjective evaluations, our social system is working better than it did at any time in the past. Yet the standard rhetoric is one of crisis and despair. There is certainly a crisis, but the crisis has to do with the ways in which we imagine the future, and our rejections of realistic aspirations, rather than with how the system is progressing objectively.

There is also an old optimism about the future. Interest in the future used to be confined to people who built Utopias, although in the last century or two much of that interest has been devoted to the construction of Dystopias. A Utopia is, in Greek, literally, 'nowhere'. If you spelled it 'Eu' it would mean 'a good place'. Almost no one has written an Eutopia in quite a while. But a Dystopia is a 'bad place', and *1984*, *Brave New World*, and many similar recent efforts are characteristically Dystopian fantasies about the future.

Of course, there are other people who are interested in the future. There is the 'theology of hope'. There is an interest in eschatology – final things. There are people who are concerned about whether God has promised us one kind of future or another. And in most societies we will find beliefs relating to this issue, with current history seen as a static, endless process in which the condition of man doesn't change, but in which finally, at the end of history, there will be a period of salvation or a return to the happy hunting grounds – some way in which man is lifted out of history. Western industrial society is almost unique in having a concept of secular, material progress which, in forms such as economic growth, technological advancement, upward mobility, and self-improvement, is an assumption about the future which is central to the social system and to most people in it.

As I've said, the future has not yet presented us with data, and there is no way we can study it directly. But that doesn't mean we are powerless to form expectations about it. Obviously we do, all the time. We couldn't conduct our daily lives or make the simplest plans or decisions if we didn't have some reasonably good expectations about the future, which have to do not only with the fact, or, more accurately, the probability that the sun will rise tomorrow, but also with subjective probabilities concerning the way people will behave toward us, and various other expectations about the future that we hold with more or less confidence, and that are based, more or less, on experience.

Similarly, we can look around and see some of the things that have been changing in our society, and then ask ourselves to what extent it is likely that these changes will continue.

This does not make us 'slaves to projections'. It merely means we are asking an intelligent question: If something has been going on, is it more likely to continue or to stop?

We see, for example, that there has been economic growth. This tends to be about 4 or 5 percent in real terms each year in most Western countries. Many of the underdeveloped countries which are now achieving some sort of take-off are doing much better. Japan has been achieving a rate of 10 to 14 percent in annual economic growth for two decades. The fact that this growth occurs is a continuing social phenomenon, and the burden of proof is on those who would argue that a period of growth which has gone on for some time will now stop. There has to be a reason for it to stop, a new factor, because on the basis of business as usual it would continue. If next year people continue to do the things they have been doing this year, including innovating in science and technology at the rate they have innovated up to now, then next year technological and economic growth will continue.

It's also true that population growth in most countries will probably continue. We know a good deal about the range of growth rates to be expected. The kinds of mistakes that are made in demographic projections are rather small compared to the basic fact that we tend to get growth rates somewhere between zero and perhaps 3 percent for most countries. Whether it's zero or 3 percent, of course, makes a huge difference in the growth of living standards.

Technologies also grow at similar rates, at compound interest, at exponential rates, so that what you have at the end of any period of time is a function of what you had during that period, and represents some proportional increase. This shouldn't be too surprising, because what we get out of a technology is, crudely speaking, a result of the amount of social activity that is carried on in research and development in that field. Yet in another sense, this long-term smoothness is extremely surprising, because, as we know, technology proceeds by surprising inventions, accidents, serendipities – discoveries made by accident while looking for something else – and synergisms – innovations put together so that the combination is more important than the sum of its parts; so that all sorts of things are that specifically unpredictable combine to make up the progress of technology. Yet, if we look back at the overall pattern, we see there has been a steady growth, and we can even say what the interest rate has been, and probably will continue to be.

Perhaps the most striking example is the rate of growth of computer technology. If we look at the capacity of computers to process information, that is, the amount of information they can handle times the speed with which they can handle it (which is to say the memory capacity divided by the add time), going back to the first Harvard Mark I computer in 1944, and taking all the major machines which have been introduced to the market subsequently, it turns out that this technology has been growing by a factor of 10 every two and a half years, remarkably steadily. If at any point in the past you had learned to expect that you would get another factor of 10 improvement in your computer capacity in the next two and a half years, you would have been right. If you have that expectation today, you may well be right. In fact, the burden of proof is really on the person who argues that something has now happened to computers so that the twenty-six-year rate of growth will no longer continue.

Of course, by definition, no rate of growth can go on forever, or it will expand to fill the universe. Every growth rate we know about will top out. The question is, when, why, how, and under what circumstances? The computer example illustrates several important points. Notice that this growth rate could not have occurred had it not been for a series of technological innovations which in retrospect came along at a regular rate, but which could not have been anticipated in detail. One example – perhaps the most important – is the transistor. If the transistor had not been invented, the growth rate for computers would probably have topped out long ago. And yet if we had told the Harvard Mark I computer people in 1944 that we expected a growth rate of a factor of 10 every two and a half years because someone would invent a device like the transistor, they would have told us that the device we were describing was contrary to the laws of physics and could never be invented. In fact, it was the common belief in 1944 that a transistor-like device could not be produced.

This method of projecting technological progress in terms of some general figure of merit, called an 'envelope curve', is one of the few forecasting techniques that have yielded useful results. There is currently an excessive interest in methodology for its own sake, however. One reason is that many people have learned to think of methodology as a kind of black box which you can crank up and then it will go to work on your problem for you and you won't have to think about it at all. So that when people have invented, for example, interesting scenarios, interesting narratives of the kinds of things that might happen in the future, the next thing that happens to them is that they are asked: What is your methodology for constructing these scenarios? And they are expected to have a series of rules so that anyone can make up a scenario by following the rules, without having to consider what it is about the scenario that is really plausible, interesting, or distinctive. Am I focusing on an important problem? Am I learning anything by following this train of thought? If you do not ask questions like these, you simply do not know what you are doing, and no methodology can help you.

Similarly, there is a great tendency to talk about 'as if' systems; to say it would be desirable 'if' we understood the social system. People therefore sometimes make diagrams which are very crude metaphors for the social system. Sometimes they even make a flow chart; it may look a lot like plumbing when they get through. Or they 'simulate' the 'system' on a computer, and get overwhelming quantities of print-out as they play games with the hypothetical variables. Then they often forget that what they have is at best only a crude metaphor for the social system and go on to analyze in some detail the behavior of the system which they have now described. But it's a purely hypothetical system, existing only in their own imaginations, corresponding only very crudely to complex realities. We need only look at the literature of social and political analysis and at the attempts made by many extremely intelligent and well-intentioned people to analyze social problems by making formal models to see how often an imaginary piece of plumbing or set of equations is mistaken for social dynamics, or urban dynamics, or even world dynamics. As a step in refining our ideas about how the world works it is useful to make our assumptions explicit and then to test them; but to mistake our assumptions for realities and to draw 'counter-intuitive' policy inferences from them may be directly misleading as well as useless.

When will energy resources be depleted? At what point will the run-off from the intensive fertilization required by the high-yield grains reach the point where eutrophication of the oceans becomes a major consideration which one must balance against the gains in food production? There are people who have argued very positively that they know the answers to such questions. What I am suggesting is that we do not know the answers to those questions, and that while they are certainly worth asking, we ought not to put too much hope in getting the answers very early, and in the meantime we ought not to jump prematurely to drastic conclusions on the basis of flimsy hypotheses about what the answers may be.

What we really need for dealing with the future is not so much this kind of systematic, parametric analysis, although somebody ought to be doing it as basic research for future (not current) applications. What we need most is better techniques for dealing with the unexpected. We need to make analyses of contingencies, to think through what we would do 'if', and we have to bear in mind that most of the 'ifs' we spend time thinking about will not take place, and, often enough, some other 'if' that we didn't think about will take place instead. Nor does being caught by surprise necessarily mean our planning was inadequate, or that we need a better 'methodology'. So many things happen to us personally as we go through life, and to all of us in a complex system like a society, that many of those things are prospectively highly improbable. The numbers involved, the 'n' is that large. We have all had the experience, for example, of walking down a street in some strange city and meeting some one we know who also doesn't live in that city and thinking, 'What are the odds against this particular meeting?' A priori, they are astronomical. On the other hand, we do pass a great many faces walking down streets in the course of a lifetime; the 'n' is very large.

I think we need a technique for dealing with the unexpected. There ought to be an academic discipline for this technique, so I've even given it a name. Because if you give it a name you have done most of what is needed to have the discipline. If you give it a name you may even be able to stop thinking about it, since it is safely classified. This happens very often, as you know. It's good to take academic names from German or Latin, but it's even better to take them from Greek, and so I suggest 'adokistics', which would mean techniques for dealing with the unexpected.

Returning to the expected, what are the major things we expect? You need at least a standard case, to begin with, where affluence continues to increase, population continues to increase, technology continues to develop and people change how they feel about these things and what they do about them in accordance with hypotheses we have about what motivates people.

Let's go back to the difference between Western society and the societies that are static, traditional, where the life of man doesn't change. It seems to me that the fundamental characteristic of Western society, and of the attitude toward change, toward ourselves and toward our environment which creates these changes, is something I would like to call 'manipulative rationality'. This is a rather important point, because the *reason* for the changes taking place in our society has a lot to do with what the changes will mean to us as they do take place. By 'manipulative rationality' I mean our tendency to think rationally, in terms of logical relationships of means and ends, and then to behave manipulatively, by which I mean the tendency we have to intervene in events, to act so as to change things. If one doesn't like a situation one thinks through some way of improving it. We can get higher yield in grain, we can reorganize an organization, we can make all kinds of inventions, we can intervene in our own selves through surgery, through psychotherapy, through drugs. The characteristic attitude of our society is not to be satisfied with any situation, and to think through some way to try to improve it. This clearly is at the root of our economic and tech-

nological progress – and also of much of our current dissatisfaction with that same progress.

This characteristic does not exist to the same degree in
primitive societies. For example: Suppose you approach a
man in Polynesia who is building a dugout canoe. You ask
him, 'What are you doing?' and he says, in effect, 'I am doing
the canoe building ritual.' You ask, 'Why are you doing it?'
and he answers, 'Because it's that time of year. We've done
the canoe building dance, we've sung the canoe building
song, and now it's time to do the canoe building.'

You have manipulative rationality, you think functionally,
and so you analyze the system in which he is operating and
you say, 'Now, aren't you really building that canoe because
your people need another boat with which to go out and
catch fish and bring in some more food?'

He has no difficulty in recognizing that those effects will
occur as a result of his activity, but those effects are not his
reasons. (As Dr. Borlaug pointed out, they can become his
primary reason. He can change if given enough incentive,
and the number of traditional societies left around the world
is fast decreasing for that reason.)But until that change occurs,
those are not the main reasons our Polynesian man is building
a canoe. If they were, and if he thought the way we think in
the West (by 'the West' here I certainly include the Com-
munist countries of Eastern Europe, and Japan, and any
other industrialized country) he'd ask other questions. He'd
ask: 'Is there some better way to build this canoe? Should we
be doing so much fishing from small boats or should we
spread out some nets along the shore? What are the long-
term trends affecting our fishing grounds? Has anyone stud-
ied the food chain of these fish? Has anyone taken the temperature of these waters? Has anyone projected the political
and economic development of other countries in order to

estimate whether or not they may intrude on our fishing grounds? For example, what is happening to the Peruvian or Japanese fishing industries and are they likely to come in here in the foreseeable future, and if so, can we apply now to the Ford Foundation for a Grant-in-Aid so that we can train one of us to represent us at the UN or some other appropriate forum with respect to this contingency?' These are the kinds of questions that we ask in industrial societies. They just don't get asked that often in a traditional society. If they did, the society would not remain traditional.

The difference is only a matter of degree. Most of the things we do are done on a perfectly prescribed, ritualized basis and that's really as it should be. We've all seen things like long-range planning rituals done; we've seen research rituals conducted, especially where there is a lot of 'methodology', where people did not really know why they were inquiring into the problem that way, but that was the way one inquired into that problem. You in this audience have probably seen education rituals conducted with no one asking, 'Is there some better way to achieve the results we want?' But some part of the society, some part of the time, is asking the question: 'Is there some better way to do it?'

Most of the things we do we necessarily learn by being shown how. It would be too complicated to learn them any other way. A very simple example is tying one's shoes, which we all generally learn to do by the age of four or five or so by being shown how. If we lived in a society where no one had learned to tie his shoes and suddenly there was a new requirement that we invent a knot which would have the right properties – easy to make and holds fast when pulled at one way but releases instantly when pulled at the other way – and we had to commission a research project and get some mathematical topologists to furnish us with the proof that this knot would have the desired characteristics, and some chemical engineers to generate the fabric, and some managers to plan the manufacturing and distribution arrangements, etc., it would be a rather tedious and expensive process. As we become a society that relies more and more on this manipulative rationality for working out new solutions for social and political problems, we are more and more in the position of people who can no longer be shown how, because the requirements have changed, but who now must think their problems through more fundamentally. It's a very tough proposition, and it's part of the dissatisfaction we have with the very real progress we have achieved; part of the malaise that exists in spite of the fact that in real terms the system works surprisingly well, better than ever before for more people than ever before.

Let me illustrate this a little more. At Hudson Institute we do policy studies; for example, we may do a study for a government department like Housing and Urban Development and ask what is the relationship between housing programs on the one hand and urban development policies on the other. This requires looking at the system of which housing programs and the developing cities are a part and asking what happens when you push one part of this system. What else moves? One can imagine it like a mobile; when you push one element, everything else moves, sometimes in ways that are very surprising and 'counter-intuitive', at least until you understand the system.

One of our people had a very revealing experience. This young man was a very good analyst of complex systems. He came home one night and he was very much surprised. He saw that the dinner table was set with the best tablecloth, the best china, the best silver, there were flowers on the table, there was a bottle of champagne cooling in the ice bucket next to the table, and although he was late for dinner – he was frequently late – his wife was there in her best dress and smiling. He realized at that point that it was his anniversary and he had forgotten all about it. But he had an idea.

He said, 'Darling, it has been my experience at work that whenever a study is done of some ongoing system that is functioning effectively, the conclusions of that study tend to support the continuation of that system.' She didn't know what he was talking about, so he went on. He said, 'What I mean is, let's now do a systems analysis of our marriage. That's the best way we can celebrate our anniversary. We'll do it very informally. We'll each take a sheet of paper and we'll each make a list of every parameter of this system that's important to us, either positively or negatively, and then we'll rate ourselves on all those dimensions. We'll have to give each one its proper weight. For example, the kind of thing you could list is the fact that I'm so often late for dinner, but, obviously you can't give that a very large coefficient. That should be given a small weight because, as you know, I'm very busy. On the other hand, the fact that you cannot park the car very well and we may get repair bills now and then is a good deal more serious and I intend to rate that more heavily. But let's not quibble about that. We'll each make our own list and we'll put down everything that's of any importance. Then we'll add up all the ratings and we'll get a score that represents the performance of our marriage as a system. That by itself doesn't tell us very much, because a fundamental principle of policy analysis is that you do not understand any of your options until you have compared that option with all the alternatives. We can't take the case in which we never got married, because lots of things have changed. We can, however, take the case in which we immediately get divorced, and in Column B let's rate that situation according to the same variables. Then we should take some alternative marriages. Now, I don't want you to imagine any hypothetical cases, because you know how unrealistic you can be. Let's take some real cases, friends of ours. You could take Bob and Ted, and I might take Carol and Alice, for instance, and we'll imagine what it might be like to be married to them, and we'll rate those marriages along exactly the same variables. After we've added up all the scores we'll see just how lucky we are. The study will support our marriage-system for its continuation until next year when we can celebrate again with another re-evaluation.'

So, he set to work very happily and she left the table crying. He sat there for a long time wondering what he had done wrong. He was not the kind of fellow who gave up easily on an intellectual problem, so he did think it through and the next day at lunch he told some of us about it. He said, 'I finally understood the mistake I made. It was that I had never done a preliminary feasibility study. If I had done that, I would have been able to weigh the value of the study as a contributor to the rationale of the continuation of the marriage, on the one hand, against the disutility of subjecting our marriage to explicit, rational analysis.' That's right; there was a disutility in subjecting this commitment to analysis, which implies that the commitment has some utility which can be weighed against the disutility of questioning it.

In the primitive society we spoke of earlier, a commitment is backed with the moral and spiritual force of the community, including its super-natural powers. It is not subject to analysis and it's not something that has a utility. It is an absolute, simply not subject to revision. In our society, although I have deliberately given you a parody, anything is potentially subject to this kind of reevaluation and reassessment.

We need only reflect, for example, on the kind of debate

which took place in the New York State Legislature before the liberalized abortion law was passed last year, and look at the grounds of the discussion – not at the result, nor at which argument was right, but just the basis of the discussion. The principal issue seemed to be whether legalizing abortion was more conducive to the net result of human happiness than keeping it illegal. Now, it wasn't very long ago that the discussion would have been very different. Suppose someone had made this case: People will be better off if abortion is legalized, for many reasons: 1) People feel they have a right to decide what is going to happen to them, and they will be much happier if they can make this decision legally. 2) A lot of medical and emotional harm is done by illegal abortions and these harms could be eliminated. 3) We have a population problem; if the number of births is to be reduced, we should certainly start by eliminating unwanted ones. 4) It's well known that unwanted children don't get brought up in as healthy an emotional atmosphere as children who are wanted and loved by their parents. One could spell out these reasons and more, and make the case that people will be better off if abortions are legalized.

The answer to this case in the past would have been, 'It's against God's law.' Then the proponents might say, 'But God's law in this case is interfering with human welfare and happiness, as we have demonstrated.' And the answer to that would have been, 'But that's not relevant. God didn't promise welfare or happiness. God imposed a spiritual and moral law.'

Now, that argument was hardly heard in the current debate and it's one which is less and less heard in our society. I'm not saying it should be; I am not really discussing abortion at all. I am simply pointing to an important social change which I think is at the crux of many of the dilemmas of progress that we are now getting into – a continuing change from a religious-traditional society to a manipulative, rational, secular, humanistic society.

The argument which was heard in the New York debate was: 'You are right about the unhappiness caused by keeping abortion illegal, but on the other hand, there are lots of ways in which people will be less and less happy if you legalize it. Legalization will be conducive to conduct which will lead to greater unhappiness on the part of those people who indulge in it, it will make the protection accorded to human life more difficult to administer, etc.' The argument became one in which both sides tended to share the assumptions of manipulative rationality in secular, humanistic terms. Even if the legalization of abortion had been defeated, the terms of the debate would have made it clear that we are less and less the traditional society we once were.

I said that in our standard case we can expect to grow more affluent, just as our affluence has increased in the past. Here is a great paradox of affluence: as we become more affluent, we tend to value less and less the things that the economic system produces. One of the results of our growing affluence has been to produce a small, but important, segment of a generation of college students, and to some extent of college teachers, who tend to come from upper middle class, affluent backgrounds and who view our economic system with a rather elitist contempt. As technology has advanced and affluence has increased, we have moved away from a reliance on tradition, authority, and God's will as interpreted by whomever. We moved first, in the 19th century, to an orientation of conscience, where we were concerned with organization, doing the right thing, and being a constructive citizen. We then moved to an orientation of reason, where all these things had to be calculated and balanced. At best this orientation was able to synthesize what was good in these other orientations; at worst it was a kind of rationalizing and indecision and scientism. And, now, an important part of the country, a much smaller part than the media would have us think, but nevertheless important, primarily because of the interest of the media and the best educated segments of the society, has moved from conscience to reason to the virtues of impulse. I am referring here to Freud's distinction among conscience, reason and impulse as primary sources of energy in the psyche. These virtues of impulse, having to do with joy, love, freedom, spontaneity, and creativity, are the dominant virtues in the ideology of many young people, of many intellectuals of any age and increasingly of many businessmen and other conventional citizens.

Beyond impulse, there is even a small group which has found a new religious orientation, one of transcendence, but which is also opposed to all distinctions. In this orientation there is a mystic unity with the cosmos; there are no distinctions between parent and child or teacher and student; authority and tradition have no legitimacy; and 'expanding' the consciousness is assumed to be an unmixed good. One might ask the question, 'Why is the consciousness better expanded, especially if it is to be expanded to the point where its boundaries are lost?' But in the view of this ideology it is a positive benefit to break down all distinctions, especially all structure and all authority. This march – God's will or tradition, to conscience or organization, to reason or rationality, to impulse or fun, to transcendence or anti-structure–makes a certain amount of sense if you see that economic necessity has a decreasing hold on people. As we solve our reality problems we decrease the incentives people have had to deal with them, and people move to more subjective concerns.

As we know, there are many serious problems of scarcity

outside the U.S. and there are similar difficulties in the less developed sectors of the U.S., but it is easy to lose sight of these in the upper-middle-class, affluent ideology where one's inner consciousness is really the most important issue. In the 1930's when someone dropped out of college he did so to find a job, not to find himself. In some ways it is always easier to find a job than to find a self. The former is an objective problem and you know when it has been solved. The point here is that solving one set of problems gives rise to a new set. Solving the problem of poverty gives us the problems of affluence and the corresponding alienation that tends to go with it.

There are so many technological prospects which will give us new social problems that it would be tedious to go through a list, but let me just mention a few. We know about the results of industrialization in creating pollution. We know the dangers of much current research in the biomedical sciences which has the prospect of giving us decisions to make which we don't know how to make. Some of them are relatively trivial, such as who should get organ transplants, and when should the donor give them up? The latter is a serious problem. Death has been redefined in certain jurisdictions in order to deal with this issue. Difficult borderline cases have arisen under these changing and conflicting standards. There are even more serious consequences of this kind of research. It would obviously be desirable to be able to alter some genetic information and to eliminate various kinds of hereditary defects, to breed better generations of human beings, but then we would have to deal with a very difficult problem, of deciding what kind of human being is really better, beyond eliminating the defects which there is consensus on eliminating. Should people be brave or good or kind or clever or wise or handsome, or what? People have never been able to decide on what the proper mix of these characteristics should be. Suppose we gain the capacity to influence these outcomes, a not impossible situation: who will then decide? With what consequences?

In almost anything we look at we see suddenly some major disadvantage, some major new problem which will arise if we succeed in solving the very problem we have been trying to solve all along. Take weather control. We'd like to eliminate the devastation that hurricanes cause, for example, on the Gulf Coast and the East Coast, but if we can divert the storms, where shall we have them go? How do we solve that problem? Suppose you're the director of the weather control project and your staff tells you there's a storm in the Caribbean which looks as though given the forces in the system it can either go up the coast, where it will do so many billion dollars worth of damage but will take very few lives because the people can be evacuated, or, alternatively, it can be diverted out into the Caribbean, where it will do much less property damage because the people on those islands for the most part don't have much property, but it will kill a lot more people because they can't get away. Of course, most of the people on the Caribbean islands are not Americans and there are various other characteristics of the situation that are described to you. Has anything that's been said so far helped you make this decision? Would you like to say what your trade-off ratio ought to be between lives and property? It's not an unprecedented decision. Suppose you were deciding what ought to be spent on safety in mines, or on safety precautions in building any skyscraper or bridge, or how rough an army training program ought to be, or whether the society can afford to rely increasingly on the private automobile for its transportation, at 50,000 deaths and 2,000,000 injuries per year. In any number of decisions there is an implicit trade-off ratio between lives and property; it's a very commonplace thing. We can make a list and tell you what the numbers are. Do you want to do it with weather, too? People are working very hard to put themselves in a position to enjoy making that decision. We are able to make more and more decisions, and enjoying them less and less. One could go on.

Let me come back to the title I chose, 'Faust's Progress'. I think I've said enough to indicate the general theme and to indicate the connection of this with methodology for shaping the future. How you look at the future, what you look for, what you try to expect, how you try to think through what you might do about what you can expect, all depends very much on the meaning it has for you.

The future has had different meanings and the concept of progress has had various meanings at different times in our history. We have many poetic and mythic insights. You will remember it was the apple of the tree of knowledge of good and evil which resulted in the expulsion from the Garden of Eden. Prometheus brought the gift of fire and was punished for it. Icarus tried to precede the Wright brothers, but he tried too hard, his wings melted and he fell into the sea.

During the Middle Ages people were very clear on this issue. There was a legend then of Faust, a man who had extraordinary knowledge and power, and it was very clear to the medieval mind that extraordinary knowledge and power meant a bargain with the devil and that Faust would be condemned to eternal damnation. During the period of the Enlightenment and the beginning of the Industrial Revolution, Goethe rewrote the Faust legend in a very characteristic way: Goethe's romantic Faust made a different bargain with the devil than the medieval Faust had made. He asked, first of all, to be given powers he would never grow tired of, and his bargain was that if he ever became satisfied, at that point the devil could claim his soul. He negotiated a long contract with the devil. I'll give you a typical clause in his contract so you get the flavor of it. He asked the devil, 'Could you supply me with the sort of young lady who, with her head on my shoulder, will already be flirting with my neighbor?' And the devil said, in effect, 'Why the devil would you want that sort of girl?' He said, 'Because I don't want to become too complacent; I want to go on and on through a very long series of conquests.' And the devil said, 'All right, if that's the kind of girl you want, I can supply that kind in large numbers.' So they agreed on that and on a great many other things, and Faust became a great modern figure. He became a great entrepreneur, architect, manager of large projects. One of the things he did was to clear an area, build dikes, and settle people on it, but the dikes were not perfectly secure because that wouldn't be good for the people, and this was, again, characteristic of him.

Finally, toward the end of the play, he says to the moment before him, 'Abide with me, thou art so fair,' and at that point the devil comes in to claim his soul. But then angels intervene and they say, 'It's true that he made this contract, but he's really been so good at it; he's carried the whole thing off with such flair; he's been really a heroic figure, so we'll save him just the same," and they do.

Now, here we are in the last third of the 20th century. We no longer believe that if we get extraordinary knowledge and power we are for that reason necessarily doomed. On the other hand, we no longer think that if we can only carry it off in a very grand way we'll almost certainly be saved. We've made a different bargain with the devil, and this bargain has a hidden hook on it which I am afraid we may not have paid enough attention to. Our bargain – I think we all know what it is by 1971 – runs like this: We want the knowledge, we

want the power, and to get them we will take responsibility
for the consequences. If we pollute the environment, we'll
figure out how to clean it up. If we make weapons of mass
destruction and pursue an arms race, we will learn how to
keep it under control. If we do large-scale data processing
and there are possibilities of invasion of privacy, we will work
out safeguards. Whatever it is, we know there's a problem,
we'll work out the solution to that problem, too. That's our
bargain.

Now, in the first place, it's going to be very hard to keep
that bargain. There are too many 'second-order' consequences
to the things we are doing. And we not only have to solve
most of them, we have to solve them all or we're going to be
in some serious kind of difficulty. But that's not the hidden
hook, because we sort of know that. The hook is this. As we
solve these problems and as we go on and on through this
acceleration of progress we become more and more the kind
of society which is committed to manipulative rationality as a
way of working out the kinds of people we are. And the
changes go on and on. We are like mountain-climbers on an
untried route: the fact that we have passed points of no return,
and cannot go back, doesn't necessarily mean that there is any
place further we can go successfully. Yet, it goes on and we
find ourselves more and more in the situation of my systems
analyst on his anniversary, trying to think things through, but
not being quite good enough at it, trying to invent new ways
to tie his social shoes, but not doing it quite well enough.

This is not the kind of problem that necessarily leads to the
extinction of the species or to the destruction of civilization,
although it can lead to those things, but it does lead to a great
deal of dissatisfaction with the kinds of progress we do succeed in making. This may well be an overriding philosophical
issue in the next decade or two. I think we are going to be

preoccupied increasingly with questions of meaning and purpose. Dilemmas and fundamental philosophical issues once again will seem important. Shallow Utopianism, particularly the shallow technocratic Utopianism that held that there was a technical solution for every problem, is going to be increasingly discredited, but we may not have a satisfactory substitute for it.

This sort of philosophical problem which may preoccupy a generation is not normally 'solved' in any way. What usually happens is that the problem is survived until some other issue comes along that appears more important. This may be the best in some ways that we can hope for.

It is also possible we may solve it. There may be some way of reinstating the values of reason, of finding a viable kind of rational, liberal, democratic solution to these problems. If there is, it will not be easy to find or to use. But finding it is not guaranteed. I once saw a cartoon that showed a dinosaur giving a talk to a group of dinosaurs and what he was saying was, 'Fellow dinosaurs, obviously we shall succeed in adapting to the coming changes in climate, for if we do not succeed, we will not survive.' Those were his last words.

JOSEPH SITTLER

The perils of futurist thinking

DR. JOSEPH SITTLER *has been a Professor of Systematic Theology at the University of Chicago Divinity School since 1957. He holds an A.B. from Wittenberg, College, Springfield, Ohio, and a B.D. from Hamma Divinity School, Springfield, Ohio. In addition to graduate study at Oberlin, The University of Chicago, Western Reserve, and the University of Heidelberg, Germany, Dr. Sittler has been awarded honorary degrees by eight colleges including Notre Dame, Gettysburg, and Loyola.*

Born in Upper Sandusky, Ohio, Dr. Sittler was pastor of the Messiah Lutheran Church, Cleveland Heights, Ohio, from 1930 until 1943.

In 1943 he became Professor of Systematic Theology at Chicago Lutheran Theological Seminary, a position he held until he joined the faculty of the University of Chicago in 1957.

Dr. Sittler has been very active in the Church. He was a delegate to the Ecumenical Conference on Faith and Order in 1952, 1963, 1965, and 1966; a delegate to the Lutheran World Federation in 1952 and 1957; and the World Council of Churches in 1954 and 1961.

He is a member and past president (1951) of the American Theological Society; and a member of the Academic Council, Ecumenical Institute for Advanced Theological Study, Jerusalem.

His published works include: The Ecology of Faith, The Care of the Earth, *and* The Anguish of Preaching. *He has given chapel talks at over 25 colleges and universities including Dartmouth, Vassar, and Princeton; and has been a guest lecturer at Yale, Harvard, Duke, and the Pacific School of Religion.*

Dr. Sittler is married and is the father of six children.

This conference is primarily for students. In my preparation of proposals, I have tried to keep that in mind. One reason for keeping that in mind also is my very modest estimation of the academic lecture. We have at my university a number of endowed lectureships. Not long ago a very distinguished philosopher came on one of these and gave a magnificent lecture. There were eight students and two professors present. The lecturer didn't seem to mind that and nobody else seemed to mind it because everybody understands what a lectureship is for. A lectureship is an academic device to pry out of a hesitant mind its best notions. And everybody knows, further, that within two months of a lecture it will be published and therefore why sit on a bad seat and listen when in two months you can sit in a good chair and read? The academic lectureship as a performance has a limited use and, therefore, each of us, I think, has in his own way understood this and has played fairly free with whatever text he proposed to bring to this Conference. I intend to do the same.

Another reflection at the beginning. This twenty feet or so that separates that table from the students really might be called a 'generation gap.' All participating symposiasts hold established positions in realms of discourse in which the data have been organized, methodologies refined, ways of thinking have acquired a certain stylized form and, therefore, because of that assumed competence we are asked to come here and contribute to the discussion. But the irony of the matter is that the very components which constitute the legitimacy of our

invitation are the very questionable assumptions which constitute the minds of the students! What the students are saying
is: maybe that's not the way to think about the world! Maybe
the way you may have got your reputations and have worked
in the past has not produced results which are so unquestion-
ably magnificent that you ought to be talking about this matter
at all. What I'm saying in a perhaps over-dramatic fashion, is
that there are certain assumptions which constitute the student
mind to which we are supposed to be addressing ourselves
which do not with equal clarity constitute the steady assumptions of the minds of those of us who are doing the talking.
So, I want to begin this morning by trying to live myself into
the mind of the student who listens and ask if there are questions which are constitutive of the style and temper of that
mind in our time which, if not made public and not exposed
at the outset, will lurk around *incognito* and haunt us in solitude
when we shall have taken the plane or you shall have returned
to your dormitories.

Such questions, the thus far unexamined assumptions of the
topic, are the ones I want to bring to the surface. They inhere
in the statement of the topic itself. First, the assumption is that
there will be a future for man. Now, despite the fact that most
persons have simply assumed the future, there have been
others (the Millerites, in upper New York State) who were
very clear about when the world would come to an end and
were occasionally disappointed that it didn't! Despite the fact
that there have been such guesses about the nature and length
of the future, this is the first generation that has questioned
the future *as such*. When I was in college I had reason, on the
ground of my previous academic performance, to question
whether I had a very distinguished future. I had worries, too,
about how to prepare for what future might present itself as
challenging. I had a good deal of worry about the number of

possibilities that were there and how to come to a choice among them. But the future as such, that there would indisputably be a future for man and for me as a person; – this was not a problematical assumption at all.

For this generation that assumption is not to be taken as an indubitable and unquestionable assumption. And while that fact ought not to stifle thought or to hamper action it does give a context for the style of reflection with which students in this generation are engaged and those of us who are talking here must attend to it. About 10 years ago there used to be a car card on the streetcars and in the buses: *Is there a Ford in your future*? The theme for this generation is: Is there a future in your future?

Now, the second assumption: Can man shape the future? Our theme, of course, assumes that he can. I want to question that. Can man shape the future in such a way as shall be ministerial both to his deepest desires and within limits and by procedures which nature will accept without reprisals? I don't think I need to beat that point out in detail; my colleagues have done that. Whoever does not sense the force of that presupposition and that question has not been looking or listening or even smelling. But having raised that question, whether man can shape the future, how shall we deal with it?

I would suggest – and I have heard nothing in this conference to cause me to modify this statement – that we are almost totally unprepared intellectually or emotionally, to take that question seriously as American men and women. For 150 years we have thought and acted as if that issue were either clearly solved or on the way to solution by the scientific and technological enterprise, or that it was an unimportant or uninteresting issue. Put it another way: We have assumed that man has historical consciousness, and as dynamic historical operator has displayed such ingenuity and managerial potency

that we have brought the world-as-nature under such knowledge and control as to bring it within our decisions about the
world-as-history. And therefore we can now regard the world-
as-nature as a latent resource to be managed as our decisions
as historical beings decide. To put it still another way: The
world-as-history now stands over against the world-as-nature
in such a way that we regard nature as being acquiescently
subsumed under the world so comprehended.

I find that massive assumption still largely unquestioned by
many members in the natural and the scientific disciplines.
And I might add parenthetically that what the members of
those disciplines still do not question at a very grave level is
exactly the kind of question that's being asked in *Hair*, *Easy
Rider*, *Five Easy Pieces*, *Midnight Cowboy*.

The first question, then, simply asks if the presupposition
of a future is unambiguous. The second question asks if our
specialized ways of investigating and speaking are not humanly, and by the empirical fact of the present embarrassments of
our world, so questionable that we must re-think our whole
way of knowing.

The third question: Shaping the future. *To shape* is a verb
that evokes images. And all the images are wrong. To shape
evokes the image in which you have a relatively inert mass
being worked upon by a worker – clay in the potter's hands,
obedient material in the painters' or architects' or engineers'
or the sculptors' hands. The image is viciously wrong; in fact,
it is a lie. If that lie remains unexposed we shall confound our
problem by such mellifluous statements as shall simply mask
the delusion the more horribly. The delusion is that historical
man can be rightly related to the world in such a way as is
supposed by the imperial word 'to shape' the future.

Despite our best efforts we continue to think nonecologi-
cally about ecology. All of our reflections upon ourselves, our

future possibilities and what might be good and fulfilling for man, will be distorted if this delusion persists. I should like to illustrate in several ways the rootedness of that delusion in our common life as well as at the rarified levels of intellectual reflection. On the day the huge tanker *Manhattan* broke through the hitherto unpenetrated Arctic ice, the *New York Times* headline read: 'Man's Ancient Enemy Overcome.' This is an instance of what Professor Hugh Iltes of the University of Wisconsin has called 'ecological pornography', and it's the more perilous because the statement is not evilly calculated. The uncalculated reaction of the popular mind disclosed in that headline puts the problem at its really deep level because considered stupidities are less disclosive of man's real problems than instant reactions are. The Arctic ice, the permafrost, the flora and the biota of the tundra have for thousands of years been a supporting eco-system. They have supported and enfolded a solid and humane culture.

The Arctic ice is called in the popular response 'an enemy'; but it is an enemy only from the perspective of the managers of the American oil industry. It is not an enemy to man, to man's world, to man's future, as any earth scientist will quickly tell you. It is one of the vastest, most exquisitely balanced, sustaining, protective, and productive structures we know in nature. Huge, but delicate; easily upset and if upset, never to be righted.

I take my second illustration from a publication called *Cacotopias and Utopias*, a little booklet published some time ago by the Center for the Study of Democratic Institutions at Santa Barbara, California. This little booklet records a conversation between a number of eggheads at that place, and Mr. Michael Harrington. Mr. Harrington in his comment speaks as follows: 'One important aspect of Utopia is that we must understand its limits. Some socialist writer, it may have been

Trotsky, said that the function of socialism is to raise man from the level of fate to that of tragedy.'

I want you to reflect upon that statement because socialistic corporate thought, which is highly managerial in its character, raises men, when it goes far enough, to the level where they see the *limits* of planning, become aware of the uncalculated permutations and novelties and combinations that grow out of the fecundity of the life of history. Experience suggests that there are limits built into the human situation which cannot be planned and would reduce the amplitude of our humanity if they could be. Mr. Harrington continues in this quite remarkable paragraph:

> 'As a matter of fact, I have thought for a long time about Karl Marx' prediction that in a society where men are no longer murdered or starved by nature but where nature has brought under man's control, there would be no need of God because God is essentially man's projection of his own fears and hopes. I wonder whether if at precisely the moment all economic problems are controlled there could not be a great growth in reflection about the transcendent rather than a decline. It's a possibility because we would then have a society in which men would not die from flood or plague or famine nor from their own idiocies about the economy; they would simply die from death. At that point the historical shell around the fact of death would be broken and for the first time men would face up to the fact of finitude.'

The first peril in futurist thinking, then, resides within the very term we have chosen to advance such thinking. *Shaping* is the fundamentally wrong term with which to address the problem. And the wrong is inescapable if we leave it uncorrected. For a methodological error perverts everything that follows. To shape the future is olympianly anthropocentric. Anthropocentricism is a proper, indeed necessary, starting place for men to begin to think; I would suggest that it is a catastrophic place from which to deal with the things they think about.

Therefore, I raise a purely formal question: Is thinking about the future, as such, in such continuity with what we mean by thinking, as to enjoy the term 'thinking' in the same sense in which we use the word when we talk about thinking about the past or the present? Is it thinking of the same order at all? Mr. Wiener reflected somewhat on this matter. This question is more than a fussy formality, for thinking about the future does not really deal with data-in-being. By definition, it cannot. Its data are extended, extrapolated, probabilistic. Such thinking may be informed reflection and as such it is both right and necessary. But it is actually discontinuous with such firsthand or remembered or recorded actuality as constitutes the occasions of thought as we commonly engage in them.

But even if this formal difficulty be admitted and the term 'musing' about the future be substituted as more appropriate, there is still another peril. It is, I think, not an incautious speculation to affirm that at the heart of our cultural crisis, and dramatically so as we confront the ecological debacle, is the strong and perduring temptation to transfer models of thought from one realm of discourse to another. Ever since Descartes a particular way of knowing and of achieving wisdom has been refined, applied, become virtually normative, and on the ground of its enormous and dramatic efficiency in penetrating and thus utilizing the structures and the processes of the natural world has become the dominant force in the creation of our civilization. One should not be accused of antirational bias if one suggests the peril that resides in this success. Michael Polanyi in philosophy, Levi Straus in anthropology, Mircea Eliade in the history of religions, Martin Heidegger in metaphysics – each in his own way has affirmed that the examination and assessment of data is methodologically perverted if data are brought under categories for assessment which are *reductionist* – the temptation of exactly the tradition which has so vast a reputation.

When a moment ago I suggested that the problem at the heart of our culture lay in this point (and I think it does, although the young from whom I have learned thus to think may not acknowledge my too formal articulation of it), I am also suggesting that at the heart of our dis-ease is a radical dubiety about the whole way of knowing and way of forming statements, and of living lives, and of making judgments that proceed therefrom. I am simply proposing for reflection a body of fact with which we are presently overwhelmed and by which men of my generation are overwhelmingly puzzled. What's going on here? The generation gap; the restlessness and anger of the young within a world and self-understanding that has been dominated by science and its child, technology; the concentration of contemporary song, short story, modern film upon the authenticity, the persistence and the promise of the natural, the immediate, and the non-utilitarian; the candor and fierce joy in personal relations; the apparent anti-intellectualism of this generation (which is nevertheless using intellectual analysis of the blunders of *my* generation with a vehemence that my generation was not able to undertake); deep dubiety about the entire value structure, and the publicly accredited and acclaimed agenda for the good life both public and personal; the acknowledgement on the part of the young that that 'good life' may be utterly incompatible with the achievement of a sane ecology; the dramatic repudiation of the myth of progress when that myth is supported by such evidence of material and technological achievements as leave the poor embittered, the sick neglected, the Chicago schools and Cook County hospital in decay while 106 millions of dollars are expended upon an exposition hall which is now a building on a shrinking public shore of a threatened lake!

All of these facts are trying to say something to us and we had better listen. Is it perhaps saying this: That in virtue of a new situation we must undertake a quite fresh transcending of the long solidified and general categories into which our ways of knowing and ways of acting have been dichotomized? This dichotomy is almost absolute. Ever since Fichte the whole university system has been cloven into *Geisteswissenschaft* and the *Naturwissenschaft*, the discourse that deals with man in the wholeness of his humanity, and discourse developed for the investigation of the structure and process of the world-as-nature.

In a recent essay Rosemary Ruether, discussing the history of evolving man's transactions with nature, affirms that a fierce and galloping negative parity has occurred. Man's technological innovations move now in an irreversible fashion, in a destructive relationship to the natural environment. Man is destroying the very basis of human and organic life; he is literally eating up the foundations upon which his life is based.

I shall not expound the data that justify such a statement for I assume our general acquaintanceship with such data suggested the theme of this conference and my colleagues have supplied more of it. What is clear is that the old walls of division across which a polite, because somewhat contemptuous, discussion between the scientific and the religious communities has taken place, must now be transcended or torn down. For such a new encounter, both the religious and the scientific communities are ill-equipped. The liberal theologians have got on so well in a pluralistic and uncritical relationship with the scientific enterprise, and they remember their burned fingers of the past too well to return to the dialogue. And the conservative or fundamentalist take the present problem as simply a kind of heavenly vindication of theology as the queen of the sciences and are tempted to think of science as simply a naughty child returning to its mother. Both of these old ways of opening the problem, locked within out-dated standoffs between an arrogant science and a defensive religion, are incapable of being usefully reopened. What we need is the reopening of a new critical dialogue whose terms are now freshly given both to the scientist and to the humanist in the matrix of ecological fact. The limitations of a single lecture do not provide much leisure to elaborate how, at the heart of the Christian and Judaic tradition, there does indeed lie an organic and holistic way of regarding man in the world which is profound and ample enough to address us in our cultural need. But reflections upon two aphorisms from St. Augustine will suggest the main lines and vitalities of what I would want to unfold had I the time for it. The first one that I want to ask you to reflect upon (and that reflection, if you take it seriously, will do more for you than anything I say) is a sentence from the famous treatise on the Holy Trinity: '*Non intradit veritatem nisi per caritatem*'... there is no entrance into truth save by love.

Augustine did not intend by that a sentimental or romantic statement about how in interpersonal relationships one opens himself to the other. His statement is based upon the conviction that there is at the basis of the world-as-nature, at the heart of the world-as-history, and at the heart of that human world which lives at the intersection of these two, a force, a meaning and a principle that became incandescent in the drama of redemption, an event of which men said, 'Behold, a whole man.' In this incarnated word, *logos*, was disclosed that which constitutes the interior life of the world-as-nature; it is but the incarnation, the incandescence and the embodiment of it. That is, history and nature, man and his life as an animal in the world of nature, as well as man in the elevation of a potentially dreaming angel, are all of a piece. And therefore, all less ample ways of knowing which ignore or dishonor the holy presence within the world-as-nature, so violate the creation that silently and slowly but with implacable judgment, this holy reality takes its reprisals when ignored or despised. There is no entrance into knowledge or truth save by love. Read for the word 'love,' respect, authenticity, regard for the structured thingliness of *things*; what G. K. Chesterton once called in a beautiful phrase, 'the sheer steeliness of steel and the unutterable muddiness of mud.'

The second aphorism plays on the Latin verbs 'to use' and 'to enjoy': *uti* and *frui*. St. Augustine discriminates and relates these when he speaks of the heart of sin. Listen. 'It is of the heart of sin that man uses what he ought to enjoy and enjoys what he ought to use.' Augustine is saying that if I do not regard the world which stands over against myself in terms of the authenticity of its thingly otherness, so that I invest it with a holy integrity over against which I must stand enjoyingly before I can sanely use, then I will surely abuse. He is saying that we must respect, care for, learn from that residency of the grace of the Creator which lies in all that has been created – learn from it, enjoy the difference, and honor its created right to be. If I do not do that I will certainly pervert right use into abuse; and when, conversely, I administer an endowment or a good gift – nature or sexuality or learning or faith – as a gift to be wallowed in egocentrically and do not put it to right use in relationship to the other, to my neighbor, to the common life of the world of men, I will certainly abuse.

Use without primal joy destroys right use, and enjoyment without use destroys continuing joy.

Precisely that is what the doctrine of the creation has steadily said for a long time. The doctrine of the creation has really nothing to do with the chronology or the structures of the physical cosmos. It is a vehement declaration that man and nature and history are in an inseparable bundle of a common destiny. The Chistian doctrine of God is a way of saying that; and it is no fault of the scientific community that the children of that doctrine have often said it so badly that the scientist could not be expected to understand what was being said. The doctrine of the creation has often been distorted by a language of bad science when it ought to have been understood as the high and holy symbolism of the nature of things.

At this point I want to read a poem; and I do that because the poem says with velocity what I am saying in a much more halting fashion. I want to introduce the poem with these comments. To correct man's relationship with nature is not just a problem of the future of his residency within the world as an economic creature. It is a question, rather, of man's own identity. It has never been possible for man to dredge up from his own self-understanding, language adequate to say the deepest things he wants to say about himself except by using metaphors from the world-as-nature. 'Now is the winter of our discontent made glorious summer by this sun of York.' 'My love is like a red, red rose.' The periodicities, the turnings of the seasons, the heat and the cold, seed time and harvest – these have evoked massive metaphors, absolutely necessary for man to call upon in any full utterance about himself. When we say that man and nature co-exist in a common bundle, that report is not simply an ecological statement of a *biological* sort. It is rather a fundamental acknowledgement that man has no being apart from nature.

And that's what Mr. Richard Wilbur says in a beautiful poem. I shall skip the first part but simply say what it is about. He calls his poem 'Advice to a Prophet'. He had apparently, when he wrote it, heard a lot of sermons from Christian pulpits giving people hell about the danger of the atom bomb and how they ought to repent, and he says, 'Don't give us all those long numbers that rocket the mind, the mind can't even take them in. Can't you find some simpler way to say what demonic thing we are doing by dealing with the world this way?' Now listen.

> Nor shall you scare us with talk of the death of the race.
> How should we dream of this place without us? –
> The sun mere fire, the leaves untroubled about us,
> A stone look on a stone's face?

> Speak of the world's own change. Though we cannot
> Of an undreamt thing, we know to our cost   [conceive
> How the dreamt cloud crumbles, the vines are blackened
> How the view alters. We could believe,   [by frost,

> If you told us, that the white-tailed deer will slip
> Into perfect shade, grown perfectly shy,
> The lark avoid the reaches of our eye,
> The jack pine lose its knuckled grip

> On the cold ledge, and every torrent burn
> As Xanthus once, its gliding trout
> Stunned in a twinkling. What should we be without
> The dolphin's arc, the dove's return,

> These things in which we have seen ourselves and
> Ask us, prophet, how we shall call   [spoken?
> Our natures forth when that live tongue is all
> Dispelled, that glass obscured or broken

In which we have said the rose of our love and the clean
Horse of our courage, in which beheld
The singing locust of the soul unshelled,
And all we mean or wish to mean.

Ask us, ask us whether with the worldless rose
Our hearts shall fail us; come demanding
Whether there shall be lofty or long standing
When the bronze annals of the oak tree close.

The ongoing discussion of the limitations to be obeyed in the realm of organ transplants in human subjects brings the matter of our discussion to a particularly dramatic point. In the 1969 spring issue of *Daedalus*, Professor Hans Jonas concludes an exacting analysis of the ethical issues in the matter of tissue transplants in human subjects with a paragraph I want to quote. Professor Jonas absolutely rejects the notion so operationally regnant in medical science that it is hardly questioned by the doctors – that is: what can be done, ought to be done! Professor Jonas denies that. He topples the notion of progress from its commanding position and in a paragraph of great power and beauty he calls us back to the primal reality that life most richly unfolds *within* limit, that in the mordant and the rich limit that constitutes experience one alone learns to love, and to use sanely, and to accept the mystery of existence.

If some of the practical implications of my reasonings are felt to work out toward a slower rate of progress, that should not cause too great dismay. Let us not forget that progress is an optional goal, not an unconditional commitment; that its tempo in particular, compulsive as it may become, has nothing sacred about it. Let us also remember that a slower progress in the conquest of disease would not threaten society, grievous as it is to those who have to deplore that their particular disease be not yet conquered, but that society would indeed be threatened by the erosion of those moral values whose loss possibly caused by too ruthless a pursuit of scientific progress would make its most dazzling accomplishments not worth having. Let us finally remember that it cannot be the aim of progress to abolish the lot of mortality. Of some ill or other each of us will die. Our mortal condition is upon us with its harshness and also its wisdom because without it there would not be the eternally renewed promise of the freshness, immediacy and eagerness of youth nor without it would there be for any of us the incentive to number our days and make them count. With all our striving to wrest from our mortality what we can, we should bear its burden with patience and dignity.

I conclude by simply hanging up a couple of aphorisms upon which I hope you will reflect long after I and my colleagues have departed. Play these contrapuntally, one over against another, in view of what I have said about the whole of existence being a theater of grace. Two statements: 'Be not anxious about tomorrow.' That statement was made by a man who did a deed and commanded its declaration in all men's *tomorrows*! He nevertheless said, 'Have no thought for tomorrow'. Could he have done the deed that both gathers up all yesterdays and blesses all the unnumbered tomorrows had he not lived according to the dictum, have no thought for tomorrow?

The second statement to play over against that is from the Old Testament: 'So teach us to number our days that we may apply our hearts unto wisdom.' Does not this suggest that limitation is the precondition of creativity; that the reality of God amidst the *mystery* of the future may be a grace?

I have made certain proposals here. First, that we shall *have* a human future only if some transcendent value is ascribed to that total existence in which man and nature and history constitute an ecological unity. Second, I have proposed that what Judaism and the Christian tradition have meant by the grace of God must find the theater of its acknowledgement not just in the forgiveness of sins and the sacrament and the sermon, etc., but in the very giftedness of the natural world as itself a theater of grace. And, third, a question: If we thus deal with the world as a grace, is this good outcome a verifiable proposition? Can one verify the assumption that the world is a residency of holiness and of grace? I would suggest that it just might be a verifiable assumption on this ground: investiture of all life with holy value and meaning is necessary for the right use and enjoyment of it. What is demanded by men in history and in nature as the absolute precondition of their future may be logically postulated as the reality of God and man and nature and history.

GLENN T. SEABORG

Shaping the future –
through science and technology

DR. GLENN T. SEABORG *is Chairman of the United States Atomic Energy Commission, having been appointed by President Kennedy in 1961, and subsequently reappointed by President Johnson and President Nixon. He also served under President Truman, from 1946 to 1950, as a member of the Atomic Energy Commission's first General Advisory Committee, and under President Eisenhower, from 1959 to 1961, as a member of the President's Science Advisory Committee.*

He was born in Michigan and graduated from high school in California. He received his A.B. degree in chemistry from the University of California at Los Angeles and his Ph.D. from the University of California, Berkeley.

Among his major scientific contributions are his discoveries, with several colleagues, of the transuranium elements: plutonium, americium, curium, berkelium, californium, einsteinium, fermium, mendelevium, and nobelium. During World War II, while on leave from Berkeley, he headed the group at the Metallurgical Laboratory at the University of Chicago that devised the process used in the production of plutonium for the Manhattan Project.

In 1951, at the age of 39, Dr. Seaborg was awarded the Nobel Prize in Chemistry (with E. M. MacMillan). He was awarded the Atomic Energy Commission's Enrico Fermi award in 1959, and has been awarded four different awards from the American Chemical Society. Dr. Seaborg holds honorary degrees from more than 40 educational institutions, including Gustavus Adolphus College (1954).

At the dedication of the Nobel Hall of Science at Gustavus in 1963, Dr. Seaborg suggested the annual series of Nobel Conferences which were inaugurated in 1965. He spoke at the second Conference in 1966 and is a member of the Nobel Conference Advisory Committee.

Dr. Seaborg is married and is the father of six children. He is an ardent sports fan, his favorite spectator sports being football and baseball.

For my own contribution I have decided to discuss the subject 'Shaping the Future – *Through* Science and Technology' and have chosen this approach for several reasons. One is that this conference is conducted in honor of Alfred Nobel, a man who had great faith in science and technology as the means of molding the future for a better life for all men. Nobel had a particularly difficult time justifying and fostering this idea because (similar to the situation we face in the Atomic Energy Commission) he personally was struggling to develop, and then distribute, for beneficial uses a form of power that was introduced destructively and bore the stigma of danger and death.

Another reason for discussing shaping the future through science and technology is that we have many people today who doubt this can or will be done – and some who even doubt we have much of a future to look forward to, much less to shape.

Yes, times have certainly changed since Winston Churchill said:

> If the human race wishes to have a prolonged and indefinite period of material prosperity, they have only got to behave in a peaceful and helpful way towards one another, and science will do for them all that they wish and more than they can dream...

Today Sir Winston's faith in science would be looked upon as incredibly naive. And there would be some who would go even further and claim that it is exactly his kind of thinking that has got us where we are today. But let me take issue with this. Just where are we today? What has been the role of science and technology in getting us there, and what will it be in the future?

We face some very negative opinions today about science and technology in particular, about man in general, and about their relationships. Broadly speaking, we are told that man is a failure and that science and technology are responsible. This attitude is expressed in many ways by many groups and individuals. There are the bands of disenchanted youths who go off to reject modern society by living in countryside communes where they move closer to nature but still need electricity, still drive to town to pick up supplies with which to live, and still depend on the benefits of that society's laws, communications and public health and medical knowledge. There are those groups who, not having gone so far as rejecting all of society, reject all of science and technology on the grounds that some of it serves military, social or political causes with which they do not agree. Yet many of these are the very same groups that clamor for the uplifting of the people of underdeveloped lands, admitting that science and technology must play a role in their advances.

And there are those groups and individuals who are just as unilateral in their critiques of science and technology from other standpoints – some claiming they are leading us toward irreversible ecological destruction, others saying they are the source of an alienation that deprives us of our humanity, and still others seeing them as forces separating us from a biological inheritance that we should retain. Yet all of these will agree, after some reflection, that science and technology have contributed to our humanity, are needed to deal constructively with ecological problems and could be directed to establish a healthy relationship between man and his environment.

There is a strange mixture of tragedy and truth in all these outlooks – and, unfortunately, a strange distortion of past history and present reality also. The young hippie, for example – the new Thoreau – who goes off with his companions to live a communal life close to nature, no matter how noble his intentions or how strong his feelings, cannot be a model for his fellowman. In his total dedication to his values he can only become a parasite, reflecting a kind of pseudo-independence from the modern world. And should this aspect of his lifestyle be emulated by all his fellow youth, social and ecological disaster would eventually follow. Contrary to many romantic notions that abound today, nature alone could not support the billions of people on earth now (and the billions due even with population control). Should this be even partially attempted, every hardship that man has suffered in the past would be visited upon him many-fold, nature and man would be devastated in constant conflict with each other, and we would see eventually, rather than the communal spirit and love projected by the young idealists, an aggressiveness and vicious competitiveness the like of which history never revealed. If you do not believe me, try projecting what the world would be like as each of the benefits of modern science and technology were removed and then all the people of the world were asked to retreat further and further into those supposedly ideal and idyllic yesteryears when men lived closer to nature.

But I dislike even suggesting such an exercise because there is a basic flaw in the 'return to nature' idea – to the idea that anything that man does scientifically or technologically is somehow 'unnatural.' This is a powerful notion, a pervasive feeling, that runs through the thinking of so many people today as a reaction to some of the problems which science and technology have created. And while there is no doubt that we have an inherent love of the natural and a need to enjoy nature's attributes, that love and that enjoyment are enhanced and highlighted today because we have the luxury of enjoying nature as a friend and not a foe. The people of the U.S. who can drive to a campsite in a National Park and set up house-keeping in a camper or tent trailer with all the conveniences of home can afford to think and feel differently about nature than those people of East Pakistan for example, some of whom, as seen in the last holocaust there, have little choice but to live or die according to nature's whims.

My main point, however, is not based merely on this com-parison of perspectives. It is based on the idea that modern man is neither acting 'unnatural' nor separating himself from nature. He is, in the broadest sense 'doing what comes natural-ly.' For if we reflect even for a moment we can realize how much science and technology are a part of nature's evolu-tionary process. How can this be so? The answer is not diffi-cult to follow. Nature has endowed all forms of life with some protective or responsive means of survival. But what has she given man in his evolution? He is most poorly equip-ped in many ways. His vision is terrible compared with a bird's. His sense of smell is inferior to almost every four-legged animal. His natural means of locomotion are relatively clumsy. He benefits from no camouflage, no claws, no large incisors, and in his birthday suit he is ill-equipped to live in most of the world's climate.

What, then, did nature give man? She developed in him a brain and neural system, and a degree of manual dexterity, that allows him to amplify his limited powers through ab-stract thought, language and the use of tools and energy. His survival and evolution are based on a dynamic interplay of these, and on his ability to grow by his adjustment to the feedback from his errors and successes. And I contend that his evolution today, through the various civilizations and societies we have seen, and into the modern global one that is struggling to be born, is a *natural* evolutionary process. Furthermore, it is a process that is moving us, not toward self-destruction, but toward a higher form of life. It is forcing moral and social growth and preparing man for what John Platt has referred to recently as a 'Hierarchical Jump' to a new level of man or mankind.

So let me reemphasize that, contrary to much that is heard today, science and technology are not unnatural or anti-nature, nor are they aberrations of human development that will lead to man's downfall. Anyone who merely compiles their errors and their human misuses in a one-sided picture to condemn and dismiss them as that, is totally lacking in vision. If man were to pursue the illusion that he could 'adjust' to nature without a constant upgrading of his science and technology he would soon be extinct. Those who would depend for survival strictly on nature's ecological balance, devoid of man's intellectual equalizers, would witness the rapid decline of man and the ascendancy of another species – most likely the insect, perhaps even the lowly cockroach who, we are told, has survived for millions of years and is still going strong.

But in stating my case in defending science and technology from this broad standpoint, I decidedly do not want to give the impression that I believe science and technology as used by human beings are unmitigated good, that all the criticism of them today is invalid or undeserved, or that much good may not result from the values of our youth's 'counter-culture' on our 'science culture.' Feedback from such a 'counter-culture' is absorbed and the best of it will have a good and lasting effect on our society. It simply is not true that our scientific-technological civilization is unresponsive to, or destructive of, our humanity. In total, it is a very human and humane enterprise that is guided by human drives and that tends to elevate, not debase, those drives. Let me dwell on another aspect of this point for a moment.

If it seems we are being told from all sides today that man is a failure, it is, ironically enough, because we are being judged in terms of a whole new set of standards in a world where almost everything seems possible – and now – almost every want, every injustice and every wrong seems unbearable. Alexis de Tocqueville anticipated this over a century ago when he said: 'The evil which was suffered patiently as inevitable seems unendurable as soon as the idea of escaping from it crosses men's minds'. This holds true with a vengeance today. And I do not say that we should not maintain that impatience as long as it drives us to act, and act constructively. In fact, a countryman of de Tocqueville, Victor Hugo, made a very cogent statement on the constructive use of this impatience when he said, 'Good government consists of knowing how much of the future to introduce into the present.' There is no doubt now that science and technology have made this aspect of government increasingly difficult.

But because we can make instant coffee does not mean we can achieve instant population control; neither can we throw our environment into a washing machine, nor can we, like a response to a cry for 'demand feeding', alter the relationship between our technological and economic systems overnight. And certainly achieving the single goal of placing a man on the moon – no matter how impressive a scientific and engineering achievement – is not to be compared with an ability to raise the 'quality of life' of 200 million people. The important thing to remember is that the combination of this impatience, those values brought on by our new awareness of conditions as measured against potentials, and the knowledge and power that science and technology can provide, represents a force that could truly elevate man.

At this point I must stress our new awareness of our environmental and human condition because it is the basis of a whole new era of scientific, technological, social and political action ahead, and because it is actually quite remarkable. As an example of this just let me point out a personal observation. In a little bookstore across the street from my Washington office they have compiled a reading list 'in ecology and related subjects' for their customers. At last count that list numbered some 260 books, most of which were published within the last three years – and these are books just stocked by this small store. Remember also that these are only books. The profusion of technical journals, newspaper and magazine articles and television and radio programs related to these subjects has now reached the proportions of a torrent of information and expression of concern. And all this cannot help but have a profound effect on the direction of our society. Eventually it should be a very positive effect providing we can maintain a balanced perspective and not allow the revelation of our problems to drive us to despair and defeat rather than the necessary constructive thought and action.

Let me make one further point on this new awareness. It seems to me that, among other things, civilization progresses through our use of a combination of hindsight, insight and foresight – with our advances depending largely on the extent to which we can emphasize the latter two. A review of all the popular material on environmental and social problems today shows that at the moment we are still very heavy on hindsight, although there is much good insight coming through now. The result is that we are still spending too much time and effort in seeking out scapegoats for today's ills and making historical comparisons which are unproductive and invalid.

In this same vein we have many people who see the past

and present through a strange pair of glasses, one that filters out our human advances as they approach the present and highlights only the 'glories of the past', giving the impression that the total condition of man is regressing. Nothing could be further from the truth – all our environmental problems notwithstanding.

But instead I urge any who doubt our accomplishments and our potential, to read a remarkable book, '*Optimism One – The Emerging Radicalism*' by F. M. Esfandiary. Mr. Esfandiary – who was born in Iran, lived in many parts of the world, worked for the United Nations, and now lives and teaches in this country – attacks the entire mythology generated by to-day's cynics. His ruthlessly realistic appraisal of days past and of how those in the underdeveloped areas of the world live – essentially still living in the past – as compared with the conditions, care and compassion of the modern world is indeed impressive. He speaks of our relationship with nature, of social conditions of the old world, of identity, alienation and violence and he speaks as one who has *lived* in both past and present.

If we want to shape the future – and particularly through science and technology – we must get out of the traps created by the despair of today's cynics or the frustration generated by unrealistic expectations. Neither condition allows us to develop the proper insight and move on to applying the necessary foresight which is so important today.

How then shall we move ahead? What should we expect from science and technology? What needs to be done to use them to the best advantage? And if this is done where might they take us? In other words, what will be the shape of the future they provide?

To answer these questions we must explore a basic dilemma of our times. That dilemma, stated oversimply is: How can we have the growth to meet expectations already generated – global expectations that seem to make virtually unlimited demands – in a world of physical limitations, many of which are already being approached? The immediate reaction to this (and it is one shared by many people today) is to stop the growth; or to be more explicit, limit population, reduce expectations, lower production and pollution and concentrate on the redistribution of material things and the 'quality of life.' This is a very natural, rational and human reaction. But, unfortunately, taken as a single prescription, it is neither a very realistic nor imaginative one. Let me explain.

Man since his earliest days has always played what is known as the 'zero-sum game.' In a limited environment – limits enforced by physical, social or political boundaries or by his own ignorance – he has had to compete or share a limited amount of resources. But as he grew in his ability to manipulate his environment, through knowledge and tools which gave him advantages, both destructive and productive, he was able to expand the sum to be divided and extend himself to new limitations. Through history – the ages of exploration, of industrialization, of scientific revolution – he was able to expand both his frontiers and expectations. During such growth the impression was gained that he was no longer playing that zero-sum game because different costs – human hardships and environmental changes – were not accounted for. But it should also be noted that each major expansion, each increase of the sum, was made possible by a major human advance in knowledge, in technology and in a new resolution of the human will to support it.

Today we have reached the end of another era of expansion, and in the eyes of many it is an end that is final and discouraging. Surveying population growth, resources depletion, environmental pollution and limitations and man's general social conditions these people tend to say, 'The jig is up. We have reached the end of the line. There is only one way to go: freeze further growth and work within the limitations of this new zero-sum, this Spaceship Earth which our new perspective allows us to see in a new light.'

When contrasted with the major feelings of only a few short years ago that the 'sky was the limit', that economic growth was synonymous with progress and that both were essentially limitless, the new attitude I just mentioned seems far more sane. And I agree that if it were simply an either/or proposition I would immediately side with those who opt for the freeze. For the natural limitations, physical and otherwise, of uncontrolled growth are obvious. And rather than blindly moving ahead into their devastating effects, rather than letting natural laws put a harsh stop to our growth, we would be better off imposing our own limits, harsh as they also might seem to some.

But we are *not* faced with a strictly either/or proposition. Economic growth and ecological balance are not necessarily incompatible. There are areas where new growth and development are essential and there are those in which they should be leveled off or even cut back. There is also a new morality being introduced into the marketplace that will allow economic values to be assigned to environmental necessities so that through a combination of regulations and incentives we can enjoy a type of human advancement neither tied only to a rising GNP nor bound to a harsh zero-growth policy. The key to this middle way, however, lies mainly in the wise development and application of science and technology. With our global frontiers seemingly closed they hold secrets to widening those frontiers, to radically expanding the new zero-sum to which we seemed to be confined.

Before explaining how they might do this let me clarify

what kind of growth I am talking about and why we must pursue further expansion in a rational way.

The idea of zero-growth is, surprisingly enough, one that appeals most to the educated middle-class American. For a combination of reasons, one of which might be his own feelings of guilt as he surveys his own abundance and environmental impact against the problems of the day, this citizen feels we must change our direction. He is sincere in his concern and willing (but probably only to a point) to make sacrifices to right the wrongs that have been perpetrated in the acquisition of his affluent society. But what he does not realize is that, for all its size and impact, if it were possible to distribute today's wealth evenly among the four billion people of the world, it would not go very far in meeting the needs and expectations that exist – not to include those of the future already born.

And simply to compare the income and environmental effects of the average American and citizen of a developing nation and use that as a guide to future action makes little sense either. To the hungry and the poverty-stricken ecology is irrelevant. Not having Social Security, or much other security, they breed for survival – to assure the perpetuation of their people and to have the necessary support should they survive to old age. So that while important programs of population control have been moderately successful they struggle against a natural instinct that could be adjusted by greater development, development that can take place through advances of science and technology without further environmental degradation and within some kind of rational economic framework.

The advance of the so-called 'Green Revolution' – the creation and distribution of new high-yield crops as supported by the Rockefeller and Ford Foundations and carried out by men such as Nobel Laureate Norman Borlaug is an example of the kind of development I have in mind. Of course, the ability to lift a people above a marginal existence to a position where they have the strength and will to further advance must be supplemented by other means of development. Energy, education, improved transportation and communication systems, and appropriate industry must be brought in. But not in the way they were introduced into today's advanced nations, for then they would repeat and compound many-fold the environmental and social problems those nations face. And here is where advances in science and technology and their application can make all the difference, can shape a new future rather than disastrously imitate the past. There is no need for today's developing nations to relive the trials of a nineteenth century-type industrial revolution and arrive at many of the technologically induced dilemmas of the twentieth century. All these pitfalls can be avoided if a truly rational approach to development is used, and with such an approach the average citizen of a developing nation can arrive at a living standard satisfactory to him, in tune with his culture and 'life-style' and not destructive of his environment. It does not have to follow, as some would have us believe, that because the middle-class American has fifty times the environmental impact of a peasant in India, that an Indian cannot achieve a life of material well-being and dignity without a comparable impact.

To understand how this is possible we might look at the other side of the coin and see how the advanced nations might be 'redeveloped' through new outlooks of science and technology.

The reason why our science and technology have, paradoxically, been both a success and a failure – why they have created the progress, expectations and problems they have – is because they and their applications have been developed and adopted in piecemeal fashion within a market economy. Until most recently in our scientific age we did not have the benefit of ecological or systems thinking – nor with expanding physical frontiers did we have the need or desire for them. Specialization seemed to gain the most productive results. Everything invented or developed was used to the limits of its profitability with its negative impact absorbed or written off, if noticed at all. And so we moved into what Simon Ramo has called the 'Century of Mismatch' with unplanned or ill-planned growth, institutions incapable of understanding or directing that growth, and leading to our current era when new limits, new interfaces and all sorts of discontinuities have suddenly seemed to hit us just as we thought we had the 'good life' really made. As I pointed out before, today we have a great awareness of this situation and from this awareness a new set of truths is emerging and new guidelines for the course of society are being written.

One of these truths is that future development cannot come about through the direct exploitation of nature or man. It must be the result of using the capital of growing knowledge, of rethinking our values and revising our priorities, of learning to do more with less by increasing efficiency, by the maximum recycling of resources, by being more imaginative and less restricted by tradition in design, by learning to manage the greater complexity that is involved in the systems thinking and action we must employ.

The need for the systems approach – the ecological approach – is an important truth in itself. If we look around us we see that almost all the problems of our age are problems at new interfaces or that take place because of a lack of integration between related forces both mechanical and human. For example, we no longer have merely a highway system, a railway system and an airways system; we have a total transportation system in which each of these components must flow together. If one ceases to function or becomes overloaded the backup immediately affects or even cripples the others. If we look one step beyond this we can see that if our energy system – or any portion of it – fails, our transportation system is imperiled, our communications are affected, our health is endangered by the failure of other services and so on in a chain reaction. Similar critical relationships exist between the chain of resources, production and waste – and at the man-and-machine interface – as the role of man continues to shift from production to services. In other words, modern civilization has an ecology of its own, and maintaining its balances as well as the smooth functioning of its parts is now essential.

The human aspects of this ecology provide other examples of why discontinuities and mismatches must be adjusted. In a world witnessing an explosion of people and human activity at the same time that an implosion of these, through urbanization and other forced contacts, is taking place, enormous potential for conflict is generated at all points where there are disparities. These disparities may be harsh physical and economic differences, they may be differences in education and opportunity, they may also be psychological and cultural differences. And today on both a global and a national scale we are seeing violent reactions to these differences in the form of rising nationalism, intensified racial strife and increased conflict over ideological differences. The resulting turmoil caused by these polarizations cannot be wished or talked away. It cannot be ameliorated by retreating to irrationality or mysticism. It cannot be reduced by rationalizing that science and technology are responsible for it and therefore should not be allowed to interfere further, or, the opposite, that they alone should be responsible for correcting a situation they produced.

The solutions I see in resolving all these related problems of our age lie in recognizing fully both the organic nature of human civilization today and its inherent relationship with the natural environment that supports it. They lie in recognizing that science and technology, the major forces behind the growth and intensification of these relationships, must be used to gain the knowledge we need to fill the important gaps in our physical and social intelligence and to adjust our discontinuities and coordinate our mismatched relationships. They lie in building the social institutions (and perhaps restructuring some of our existing ones) to direct science and technology wisely just as those institutions must extract intelligence and a certain wisdom from science and technology.

Actually, we are struggling with these solutions today, or beginning to. They seem so complex, so overwhelming at times that we wonder if we are not losing that 'race between education and catastrophe.' But I think we have at hand and are developing certain tools to help us win it. Some of these have arrived on the scene, historically speaking, virtually in the nick of time. I have often spoken of nuclear energy in this context because I believe that if we pursue its development carefully and apply it wisely it will provide a reasonably controlled population of reasonable demands with a virtually inexhaustible supply of power and at a time when we can anticipate the depletion of other sources of power. I emphasized the *reasonable* population size and its *reasonable* demands because there are those who upon hearing of inexhaustible energy blanch at the idea that it will only be used to support catastrophic growth. But if after all that we are learning these days we still believe that any technology will be used to its ridiculous extremes, or to support other obviously dangerous excesses, simply because it is there, or is temporarily profitable, then we face the greatest danger of all – literally that of lacking the collective intelligence or will to adapt to our own evolution. I refuse to believe that we are suicidal. I do not think we will go that route.

Nuclear energy, used wisely, will free man for eons from what Kenneth Boulding calls 'the Entropy Trap.' Abundant energy will allow us to save nature, not destroy it, by making a recycle civilization possible. In such a civilization only energy will be depleted and natural resources, as we advance further in our knowledge of chemistry and physics, will become the building blocks of a world in which there can be endless variety without destruction. In such a civilization, we can expand the 'zero sum' so that all men can enjoy freedom from want, learn the true meaning of security and live in dignity with their fellow man. Here are the real challenges to today's anti-technologist, environmentalist, humanist, hippie and devotee of 'Consciousness III' – help us build a world that can retain its natural beauty *and* be an endless source of human creativity.

Another technology that I believe is coming to the rescue of mankind – that may make mankind possible – is the computer. As the British cybernetics expert, Professor Stafford Beer, has pointed out, 'Society has become a complex organism, and its needs a nervous system.' We are now a global civilization that depends for its survival on a growing influx of data which must be processed into information, stored, distributed and eventually upgraded to knowledge and wisdom. Today the computer is the vital link in that system. And in addition to telling us where we are, it can help us to shape our future by giving us the means to project and examine alternate futures. Through computer models we can 'look ahead' to the consequences of various courses of action we may choose. And thus we may choose more wisely.

There are many other sciences and technologies that offer great promise for the future. The earth-orbiting satellite is one of these. Equipped in various ways, it has the potential of giving us long-term accurate weather forecasting that may save many lives and much property. It can give us vital information concerning environmental conditions, the health of crops, the state of the oceans, the atmosphere, the location of mineral resources and other natural phenomena. And it can unite the world through satellite communications, providing education and a means of sharing knowledge and culture.

Perhaps the most significant shaping of the future may yet come from the shaping of man himself – directly from the great advances now anticipated in the biological sciences. Here again, and perhaps most forcefully, we are faced with the moral challenge that science and technology create. When life itself can be directly controlled, molded and even synthesized from basic chemicals, who will determine the nature, the direction and the ends of that life? Are we preparing ourselves for such God-like responsibility? In terms of cosmic time we are approaching it almost at the speed of light. We must think and plan and work and build our social institutions to manage this and other great responsibilities that our evolution is thrusting upon us. And we must do it now.

I am pleased that this conference has chosen to discuss 'Shaping the Future.' It expresses, in spite of all the despair around us today, an affirmation in that future, a belief that we have a future, and that if we will it we can be masters of that future, not its victims. I have expressed the belief that science and technology are essential to the shaping of that future. I hope we will turn to them with a growing care and dedication and use them with increasing wisdom. If we do, perhaps Sir Winston will not have been wrong and they will provide the human race with 'all that they wish and more than they can dream.'